Easy Vegan Christmas

Easy Vegan Christmas

Katy Beskow

80 Plant-Based Recipes
for the Festive Season

Photography by Luke Albert

Hardie Grant

QUADRILLE

Introduction

It's the most wonderful time of the year! Returning from a long winter walk into a cosy, warm home. Twinkling lights, bustling high streets, carol singers and the scent of roasted chestnuts and cinnamon. Loved ones gathering for a celebration of great company, drinks and food.

Yet even the most experienced home cook can feel flustered under the pressure of cooking a festive feast for family and friends. Alongside trying out new recipes, hosting a dinner, keeping everyone entertained, and creating that perfect Christmas atmosphere, it can be difficult to relax and enjoy the seasonal festivities yourself, so I created this book for you, to ease some of the pressure with easy, fail-safe recipes that everyone will love.

Whether you're cooking for your vegan family, looking for inspiration for your first vegan guest, or simply want to add new flavours and dishes to your Christmas dinner table, you'll find fuss-free recipes to get you through the season. I've also included an 'Easy Tip' with each recipe, and I let you know if a recipe is suitable for freezing – perfect for getting ahead! You'll find handy menu planners on page 19, to take the stress out of deciding what to cook. What's more, all of the ingredients are available in supermarkets, with a focus on seasonal winter produce.

The recipes are organized into simple-to-follow chapters:

Starters & Nibbles: Choose a delicious starter, light dish, or potluck plate made for sharing with others.

The Main Event: These are the stars of the show for your Christmas dinner, with many being versatile enough to work as suppers throughout the winter months.

Sides: All the side dishes, including stuffing, potatoes and delicious vegetables to take your dinner to the next level.

Gravy & Sauces: What is Christmas dinner without homemade gravy or a full-of-flavour sauce?

Leftovers: Use up your leftovers in new recipes, to save money and reduce food waste.

Drinks: From comforting hot drinks, to sparkling celebration cocktails, there's a drink for every festive occasion.

Festive Bakes & Treats: Bake up a nostalgic treat for yourself or to give as a gift, or prepare an elegant dessert to follow your main course.

I've also provided guides on how to have a stress-free Christmas dinner (page 8) and how to organize your Christmas shopping list (page 12), to help you break free of the endless to-do list, and spend more time outside of the kitchen, where the real fun is happening.

The magic of Christmas is in togetherness and giving, and there's nothing that shows this more than a special, hearty meal, prepared with love.

Wishing you a very Merry Christmas, from my kitchen to yours.

Love, Katy

How to host a stress-free Christmas dinner

Yes – you can have a stress-free Christmas dinner! Follow these simple tips to make the day an effortless, enjoyable experience.

Keep it simple

Although you may be tempted to cook every side dish, a number of main courses, and a selection of desserts, step back and assess if this is achievable for you. Realistically, a Christmas dinner for four people can generously consist of:

❄ **1 choice of main event**

❄ **2–3 sides**

❄ **1 gravy**

❄ **1 sauce**

❄ **1 dessert**

Of course, there's no limit to how much food you can cook up, but keep in mind a budget for the dinner, how you will use up any leftovers, and if you have enough serving plates and bowls. Christmas is a time for treats and indulgence, but there's no harm in serving fewer dishes if it reduces your stress in the kitchen.

Plan it

Ask your guests if there are any particular food likes and dislikes, and note if there are any allergens to avoid. It's better to plan at this stage, rather than panic at the last minute. Put your plans on paper, so you can write your shopping list, create a budget and plan what you can make in advance. Have fun with it, and even add in some special bakes and edible gifts.

Equipment

Early in December, check that you have all of the equipment you need to make the cooking process as quick and easy as possible.

❄ A good quality Y-shaped vegetable peeler makes the job of prepping vegetables effortless. Opt for one with a comfortable silicone handle, that you can control with a light grip.

❄ Sharpen your knives to reduce the effort and time it takes to chop, slice and dice.

❄ Stock up on foil, baking parchment and freezer tubs/bags, which are perfect for storing leftovers.

❄ Ensure you have enough deep roasting tins and shallower baking trays to cook all the recipes you've planned. Stainless steel tins and trays transmit oven heat evenly, but ensure you don't over fill them – two trays are always better than one when roasting vegetables.

❄ If you're baking a Christmas cake, make sure you have a cake tin of a suitable size. I use an 18cm (7in) tin for my Christmas cake (page 170).

❄ A high-powered jug blender or food processor takes the effort out of many jobs, from blitzing soup to whipping up desserts.

Trial run

A great way to increase your confidence is to have a trial run of all the recipes, cooking them either in one go for a special supper, or one-by-one over the month leading up to Christmas. You can make any preferential changes to the recipes, and make notes of timings. You can also batch cook any of the recipes that are suitable for freezing, and pop them away until needed.

Prepare in advance

Peel vegetables up to 24 hours before you need to cook them. For root vegetables such as carrots and parsnips, you can leave them in pans of iced water overnight, and get ahead of the game by pre-boiling your potatoes and allowing them to dry off (see page 18). Lighter vegetables such as broccoli, sprouts and cabbage can be chopped and refrigerated in bowls (or if you don't have the fridge space, store them in a cool cupboard or even covered in a car boot!). Many gravies and sauces can be made in advance and kept chilled, before being reheated when you need them. To allow extra time on Christmas Day, choose recipes that are suitable for freezing, then batch cook them in advance. Defrost and reheat thoroughly before serving.

Get others involved

It's good to ask for help! Not only does this reduce your workload, but it allows guests to feel like they are having a positive impact on the day. If the idea of lots of people in your kitchen fills you with dread, or if you simply don't have the space, ask your guests to prepare a dish at home and bring it along, potluck style.

Relax!

You've planned, shopped, prepared and chopped, so pour yourself that glass of bubbly, or make a mug of Christmas tea (page 144), turn up your favourite Christmas music and enjoy your time creating magic in the kitchen!

Your Christmas shopping list

Allow a few extra special goodies to make it into your shopping trolley in December; after all, it's a time of indulgence! Keep a stock of regular staples in your store cupboard for easy, effortless meals throughout the season. These can include canned chopped tomatoes, vegetable stock, spices, canned lentils, beans and flaked sea salt.

Seasonal produce

Alongside all of the traditional seasonal produce including carrots, potatoes, cauliflower, Brussels sprouts, cabbage, clementines and cranberries, it's a great time to try some new favourites of the season including celeriac (celery root), beetroot (beets), Jerusalem artichokes, pears and pumpkin. Let your produce be the star of the show by getting creative with your main dishes, instead of vegetables just being a side dish. Eating seasonally means you'll get the best flavour, lower costs, and always have new and varied produce to try. Lemons and limes make a great addition to a festive drink, and are versatile enough to use in both sweet and savoury recipes – be sure to always choose unwaxed citrus fruits, as the waxed varieties are often coated with animal products, including shellac, to add shine, making them unsuitable for vegans.

Vegan cream, cheese and butter

There's no time like Christmas to indulge in rich vegan cream, cheeses and butter. Most supermarkets have a range of fresh and long-life single (light) and double (heavy) vegan creams, with choices of soya, oat or ones made with pea protein. There is now a wide range of vegan cheeses available, from simple cream cheeses to specialist, flavoured cheese – perfect to add richness to a recipe or for creating your own vegan cheese board. Vegan butter is a fridge staple that isn't just for toast! Use in vegan baking, for perfect mashed potatoes and for glazing vegetables. Go on, it's Christmas!

Vacuum-packed chestnuts

You'll find these handy packets of ready-roasted chestnuts available in supermarkets all year round. They save the time and effort of preparing, roasting and peeling chestnuts, with less waste too. They are versatile enough to use in main dishes such as chestnut cassoulet with sage dumplings (page 71), easy rich chocolate torte (page 166), or simply for a perfect warm winter snack.

Shop-bought pastry

Shop-bought pastry is quick and fuss-free to use, and helps you to create something delicious, from savoury dishes to desserts. Many brands of shop-bought shortcrust, puff and filo pastry use vegetable oil instead of non-vegan butter in the production, making these items suitable for vegans. This can vary from brand to brand, so always check the label before you buy. Ready-rolled pastry is the most convenient to use (no need to dig out the rolling pin).

Oils

Oil transmits the heat from the pan or roasting tray to the food for faster, more even cooking with no sticking. Simple sunflower oil or olive oil are excellent for cooking with, as they have a high smoke point without an overpowering taste – these are my choices for perfect roasted vegetables. Save extra virgin olive oil for dressing salads, or dipping breads – it has a more complex flavour, as well as being a more expensive option.

Dried fruits

Stock up on dried fruits such as raisins, sultanas (golden raisins) and glacé cherries ready for baking a traditional Christmas cake (page 170) or ten-minute figgy pudding (page 158). Dried fruits such as apricots, figs and sour cherries make perfect additions to winter stews, casseroles and stuffings, and are also a delicious addition to any vegan cheese board.

Alcohol

If you enjoy a festive tipple over the Christmas period, make sure it is vegan. Wine, beer or cider can be added to a dish to give a deep, hearty flavour; or it can be enjoyed alongside your meal. Some brands and varieties of wine, beer and cider contain animal ingredients including isinglass (from the swim bladders of fish), gelatine and eggs, making them unsuitable for vegans. Some supermarkets note on the bottle label if the alcohol is suitable for vegans, or use a trusted online source to check before you buy.

Four steps to perfect roast potatoes

The humble potato is the star of the show when roasted, with a crispy outer and fluffy, hot centre. There is no mystery or magic in cooking up these family favourites, just four simple steps for fail-safe roasties every time. Find the recipe for ultimate roast potatoes on page 87.

Step 1: The variety

The variety of potato you choose to roast really does make a difference to the final result, as you need a potato that remains fluffy, but is sturdy enough to stand up to high oven temperatures. Avoid waxy varieties as you won't get that classic crunch. Maris Piper makes the ultimate roast potato (as well as being versatile enough for chips, wedges and mash), with King Edward potatoes being a steady alternative.

Keep your roast potatoes of a consistent size, so they all cook through at the same time. Getting the size just right is important – it's better to have larger roast potatoes than smaller chunks. Larger surface areas lead to crispier outers and a softer, lighter centre to enjoy. Smaller chunks tend to get hard on the outside and soggy inside, and are at an increased risk of burning in the oven. As a rule, chop each peeled potato into 2–3 even chunks for the perfect size every time.

Step 2: Pre-boil

Boiling the potatoes before roasting them breaks down the starchy outers, allowing them to soak in the oil for the ultimate crisp-up in the oven. It also transmits heat into the centre of the potato, for more even cooking and to guarantee that fluffy centre. Potatoes that are not pre-boiled tend to have a denser centre, and a greasier texture.

Bring a large pan of salted water to the boil and boil the potatoes for 10–15 minutes until a knife can go through them with little resistance. They shouldn't be falling apart, as this stage is not to fully cook the potatoes; that happens in the oven. There's no need to add anything extra to the cooking water (some recipes call for bicarbonate of soda/baking soda) as the magic happens when the potatoes are out of the boiling water.

Continued...

Step 3: Dry

One of the most crucial steps in the process of making the ultimate roast potatoes is allowing the pre-boiled potatoes to dry before you roast them in the oven. This removes as much water as possible from the softened potato to get the outer really crispy. After you've pre-boiled the potatoes, drain thoroughly, then place back in the dry pan. With a lid over the pan, vigorously shake the pan to ruffle the potatoes, then lay them onto a clean tea towel, place another towel on top and allow to steam-dry for at least 30 minutes, or even better, overnight if you're preparing your Christmas dinner in advance. If you've simply not got the time to wait for the potatoes to dry, towel dry the potatoes and add a tablespoon of plain (all-purpose) flour, then shake in the pan to ruffle the potatoes and help absorb excess moisture.

Step 4: Oil

The oven needs to be at a high temperature, so you need an oil that can withstand the heat without developing a bitter flavour. Sunflower oil has a high smoke point and a mild flavour that won't dominate your roast potatoes. It's also versatile enough to use in vegan baking and everyday cooking, as well as being a cheap and healthy oil to use. A light olive oil is a good alternative, but save extra virgin varieties for drizzling and dressing.

Heating the oil in a deep roasting tray before adding the potatoes is another trick to getting that crispy roast potato. As a rule, 3–4 tablespoons of sunflower oil in a large, deep roasting tray will take 10 minutes to heat up in a fan oven set to 200°C/400°F/gas mark 6. You'll know it's ready when it glistens and shimmers. When you place the potatoes into the hot oil, you should hear a sizzle. Be sure to leave some space between the potatoes and try not to overcrowd the roasting tray. Turn the potatoes just once, halfway through cooking, to avoid losing oven temperature and disrupting the roasting process.

Menu planners

If you need some organized inspiration for your Christmas dining, use one of the below menus as a template for your feast. Feel free to add in additional sides, sauces and drinks, if you like.

The night before Christmas

❋ Parsnip and red onion latkes with cream cheese and chives (page 34)

❋ Smoky quiche with spinach, dill and lemon (page 57)

❋ Winter apple slaw (page 138)

❋ Mince pie Danish pastries (page 173)

❋ Candy cane hot chocolate (page 155)

Traditional dinner

❋ Buttery mushroom, chestnut and thyme wellington (page 54)

❋ Ultimate roast potatoes (page 87)

❋ Pan-fried sprouts with butter, orange and lemon (page 90)

❋ Sticky marmalade carrots (page 96)

❋ Ultimate vegan gravy (page 106)

❋ Ten-minute figgy pudding (page 158)

Light lunch

❋ Blood oranges and fennel with radicchio, capers and olives (page 27)

❋ Savoury roasted pears with red onions, sour cherries and pine nuts (page 58)

❋ Roasted harissa sprouts with dukkah (page 93)

❋ Balsamic red onion, blackberry and apple sauce (page 112)

❋ Pomegranate and rosemary punch (page 148)

Family-friendly dinner

❋ Doughball Christmas tree with roasted garlic butter (page 31)

❋ Follow the star shepherd's pie (page 61)

❋ All-in-one whole roasted vegetables (page 95)

❋ Sticky gingerbread pudding with salted caramel sauce (page 161)

❋ Spiced clementine cordial (page 151)

Winter warmer supper

❋ Spiced parsnip soup with beetroot crisps (page 48)

❋ Christmas cobbler (page 65)

❋ Roasted garlic mashed potatoes (page 88)

❋ Red cabbage with orange, cinnamon and black pepper (page 100)

❋ Mulled wine (page 152)

Bring and share party

❄ Mini no-fish bites with yogurt caper dip (page 40)

❄ Sage, onion and chestnut rolls (page 43)

❄ Orange and lemon pilaf with pistachios (page 126)

❄ Cheese and chutney bites (page 125)

❄ Chocolate orange millionaire's shortbread (page 177)

Italian-style lunch

❄ Fig, walnut and mint crostini with smoked houmous (page 37)

❄ Crispy gnocchi with creamy kale, white wine and mushrooms (page 66)

❄ Cacio e pepe cauliflower (page 89)

❄ Charred cabbage wedges with chilli, tomatoes and olives (page 99)

❄ Limoncello mousse (page 165)

Gluten-free dinner

❄ Pumpkin bisque with sage oil (page 33)

❄ Jerusalem artichoke rosti with carrot purée, crispy cavolo nero and walnuts (page 53)

❄ Roasted hasselback parsnips with apples (page 82)

❄ Pan-fried sprouts with butter, orange and lemon (page 90)

❄ Easy rich chocolate torte (page 166)

Something special supper

❄ Creamy celeriac soup with toasted hazelnuts (page 24)

❄ Brown sugar and spice tofu with split pea purée (page 62)

❄ Steamed Tenderstem broccoli with five-spice butter (page 84)

❄ Cranberry sauce with star anise and clementine (page 111)

❄ Toasted coconut and marshmallow panna cotta (page 162)

Boxing Day bash

❄ Anything-goes bhajis with coconut raita (page 130)

❄ Boxing Day balti (page 129)

❄ Stir-fried sprouts with edamame, ginger and chilli (page 134)

❄ Warm pomegranate, beetroot and mint relish (page 115)

❄ Rudolph's cherry and pretzel chocolate bark (page 178)

Starters
& Nibbles

Creamy celeriac soup with toasted hazelnuts

This simple-to-make soup is mellow and fragrant, making it the perfect dish to start your festive meal. Celeriac is roasted before being blended with rosemary-infused stock and vegan cream, then topped with toasted hazelnuts, parsley and a little extra vegan cream. The result? A creamy, nutty soup, with perfectly balanced sweetness.

Serves 6
Suitable for freezing

3 rounded tbsp chopped and blanched hazelnuts
1 medium (approximately 800g/1lb 12oz) celeriac (celery root), peeled and evenly chopped into chunks
1 onion, quartered
1 carrot, peeled and chopped
generous drizzle of sunflower oil
800ml (3⅓ cups) vegetable stock
1 sprig of fresh rosemary
200ml (generous ¾ cup) vegan double (heavy) cream, plus extra to serve
generous pinch each of sea salt and black pepper
small handful of flat-leaf parsley, to serve

Easy tip

The soup can be made up to 3 days in advance and kept refrigerated, or frozen for up to a month in advance. If frozen, defrost and reheat thoroughly before topping with freshly toasted hazelnuts.

---

❶ Add the hazelnuts to a dry pan and toast over a medium heat for 3–4 minutes until fragrant and light golden. Set aside.

❷ Preheat the oven to 180°C/350°F/gas mark 4.

❸ Arrange the chopped celeriac, onion and carrot in a roasting tray. Drizzle with sunflower oil, then roast in the oven for 40–45 minutes until tender. If the edges of the vegetables are becoming browned, place a sheet of kitchen foil loosely over the top to avoid further browning, which can cause bitterness in the soup.

❹ Meanwhile, heat the vegetable stock over a medium heat in a pan with the sprig of rosemary. Simmer for 5–6 minutes, then remove and discard the rosemary.

❺ Spoon the roasted celeriac, onion and carrot into the infused vegetable stock, along with the vegan double cream, then use a hand blender to blitz until silky smooth. Alternatively, add the stock, vegetables and cream to a high-powered jug blender and blitz until smooth. Season to taste with salt and pepper.

❻ Ladle the soup into warmed bowls. Sprinkle over the toasted hazelnuts, about ½ tablespoon in each bowl. Drizzle over a little extra vegan cream, then scatter with a few leaves of flat-leaf parsley. Serve hot.

Blood oranges and fennel with radicchio, capers and olives

Balance the sensational seasonal ingredients of blood orange and fennel with bitter radicchio and a salty, olive oil-rich dressing with capers and olives. Toss in some dill and a pinch of black pepper for a winter salad that is perfect for a special occasion, whether it be a starter to your Christmas dinner, a sharing dish at a party, or a delicious lunch anytime in December. The bitter, salty flavours are perfect to be enjoyed with any aperitif.

Serves 4

6 tbsp good-quality extra virgin olive oil, plus a generous glug

1 garlic clove, crushed

2 tbsp capers in brine, drained

generous handful of pitted black olives, sliced

2 fennel bulbs, thinly sliced

2 large blood oranges, peeled and sliced into half rounds

1 head of radicchio, small leaves left whole, larger leaves roughly torn

small handful of fresh dill, chopped

sea salt and black pepper

Easy tip

The garlicky caper and olive dressing can be made up to 2 days in advance. Store in a sealed bottle or jar in a cool place, and shake before stirring through the salad.

---

❶ Add a generous glug of olive oil to a small pan and throw in the crushed garlic. Soften the garlic over a low heat for 2–3 minutes until fragrant, then allow to cool.

❷ Spoon the garlic, the oil from the pan and the 6 tablespoons olive oil into a bowl, then stir in the capers and black olives. Stir in a generous pinch of sea salt and allow to stand for 15 minutes to cool and infuse.

❸ Meanwhile, in a large bowl, toss together the fennel, blood oranges and radicchio. Stir in the chopped dill.

❹ Pour over the dressing, stirring it through to ensure it is evenly distributed. Season with a pinch of black pepper.

Maple roasted cauliflower with winter greens and ginger

Although this warming salad packs a flavour punch of sweet maple syrup, chilli heat and zingy ginger, it is light enough to enjoy before your main meal, or as a hot sharing platter at a festive party. The cauliflower florets are twice roasted – once in oil to tenderize, then finally in maple syrup to caramelize.

Serves 4 as a starter

1 large cauliflower, broken into even florets, leaves removed and discarded
1 tbsp sunflower oil
2 tbsp maple syrup
pinch of ground cinnamon
generous pinch of sea salt

For the winter greens
glug of sunflower oil
2cm (¾in) piece of fresh ginger, grated
pinch of chilli flakes
2 tbsp sesame seeds
200g (7oz) cavolo nero, leaves roughly sliced, tough stems discarded
8 Brussels sprouts, shredded
2 generous handfuls of watercress
small handful of fresh coriander (cilantro), torn

1. Preheat the oven to 200°C/400°F/gas mark 6.

2. Brush each cauliflower floret with sunflower oil and arrange on a large roasting tray (or two smaller roasting trays), leaving space between each piece so they roast evenly. Roast in the oven for 20 minutes.

3. Meanwhile, stir together the maple syrup and cinnamon. Carefully remove the roasting tray from the oven and brush the maple mix over the cauliflower. Drizzle over any remaining mix, then return the tray to the oven for a further 10–12 minutes until caramelized and golden. Season with sea salt.

4. To make the winter greens, heat the oil in a wok over a medium-high heat and throw in the ginger and chilli flakes. Toss for a few seconds, then throw in the sesame seeds, cavolo nero and shredded sprouts. Stir-fry for 4–5 minutes until the leaves have softened and are a vibrant green.

5. Spoon the greens onto a large serving plate, and scatter over the watercress and coriander. Spoon the roasted cauliflower over the greens and serve hot.

Easy tip

If you don't have cavolo nero available, kale or savoy cabbage make excellent alternatives.

Doughball Christmas tree with roasted garlic butter

Bring this tear-and-share doughball Christmas tree to the table for a fun, festive start to your meal. It's also the perfect addition to any Christmas movie night in! The doughballs use store cupboard ingredients and are easy to prepare (kids love to knead and shape the doughballs too).

Serves 4
The doughballs are suitable for freezing

300g (2½ cups) strong white bread flour, plus extra for dusting

½ tsp dried fast action yeast

2 tbsp olive oil, plus extra for greasing

For the roasted garlic butter

½ bulb of garlic, unpeeled

drizzle of olive oil

4 tbsp vegan butter

small handful of flat-leaf parsley, finely chopped

generous pinch of sea salt

Easy tip

The doughballs can be baked in advance and frozen, before being defrosted and thoroughly reheated. The roasted garlic butter has the best flavour and texture when whipped up on the day of serving.

---

1 In a large bowl, mix together the flour and yeast. Stir in the olive oil, along with 200ml (generous ¾ cup) lukewarm water and bring together to form a dough.

2 Sprinkle a clean work surface with a little flour, then knead the dough for 10 minutes until soft and elastic.

3 Lightly grease a baking tray with oil. Cut the dough into 15 even pieces and roll them into balls. Arrange on the baking tray, with 5 doughballs at the bottom, then 4, then 3, 2 and 1, in the shape of a Christmas tree. Position the doughballs close to each other but not touching (they will increase in size during proving). Cover the baking tray with cling film (plastic wrap), then place the tray in a warm place to prove for 45 minutes.

4 In the meantime, prepare the garlic butter. Preheat the oven to 180°C/350°F/gas mark 6. Place the garlic in the centre of a sheet of foil and drizzle with olive oil. Wrap the foil to secure the garlic, then roast in the oven for 20 minutes until softened. Allow to cool, then squeeze the roasted garlic into a bowl and use a fork to mash until very soft. Add the vegan butter, parsley and sea salt and stir to combine. Refrigerate until needed.

5 Increase the oven temperature to 200°C/400°F/gas mark 6. Remove the cling film from the tray with the proved dough balls, then bake in the oven for 15–20 minutes until golden.

6 Remove the doughballs from the oven and brush over a small amount of the roasted garlic butter. Serve the remaining butter in a bowl alongside.

Pumpkin bisque with sage oil

This silky bisque has a vibrant winter orange hue, an earthy sweet flavour, and the smoothest mouthfeel. Top with a drizzle of freshly infused sage oil for freshness, a little vegan double cream and plenty of black pepper. Butternut squash makes an excellent alternative if you're unable to source a pumpkin.

Serves 4 generously
Suitable for freezing

20g (¾oz) packet of fresh sage

5 tbsp good-quality extra virgin olive oil

1 medium (approximately 850g/1lb 14oz) pumpkin, peeled, seeds discarded, flesh cut into rough chunks

2 onions, quartered

drizzle of sunflower oil

1 x 400ml (14fl oz) can of full-fat coconut milk

600ml (2½ cups) hot vegetable stock

1 bay leaf

generous pinch each of sea salt and black pepper

4 generous tbsp vegan double (heavy) cream

Easy tip

I've been known to make a batch of this bisque in peak pumpkin season in the autumn, freezing it ready to serve on Christmas Day. It freezes well for up to 4 months; simply defrost and reheat thoroughly before drizzling with freshly prepared sage oil.

❶ Remove 5–6 sage leaves from the bunch and set aside. Place the remaining sage (including the stalks) into a small pan, tearing them roughly to release the fragrance.

❷ Measure the olive oil into the pan and bring to a warm temperature, over a low heat, without boiling the oil. Stir a few times, then remove the pan from the heat and allow to infuse further. Set aside.

❸ Preheat the oven to 190°C/375°F/gas mark 5.

❹ Arrange the pumpkin and onion on a large roasting tray (or two smaller trays to avoid overcrowding). Drizzle with sunflower oil and roast in the oven for 30–35 minutes until tender.

❺ Remove from the oven and spoon into a large pan. Pour in the coconut milk, vegetable stock, bay leaf and reserved sage leaves, then bring to a simmer over a medium-high heat for 10 minutes.

❻ Discard the bay leaf. Ladle the soup into a high-powered jug blender and blitz on high until silky smooth. If you're using a stick blender, blitz for longer than usual until the bisque is very smooth.

❼ Season generously with salt and pepper to taste, then ladle into bowls.

❽ Swirl in a spoonful of vegan cream, then drizzle over the sage-infused oil. Season with extra black pepper, if you like.

Parsnip and red onion latkes with cream cheese and chives

These comforting and simple-to-make latkes are a warming and casual starter, and the recipe can be easily doubled to serve more people. Serve any leftover latkes for Boxing Day brunch, either hot or cold.

Serves 4

1 medium baking potato, peeled and
    coarsely grated
1 large parsnip, peeled and coarsely grated
1 small red onion, coarsely grated
2 tsp plain (all-purpose) flour
6 tbsp sunflower oil, for frying
4 rounded tbsp vegan cream cheese
small handful of fresh chives,
    finely chopped
sea salt and black pepper

Easy tip

Freshly grate the potato, parsnip and red onion by hand using a box grater, or use a food processor for effortless preparation.

❶ Place the grated potato, parsnip and red onion onto a clean, dry tea towel, then gather up and squeeze over a sink to remove as much liquid as possible.

❷ Add the drained potato, parsnip and onion to a bowl, and stir in the flour and a generous pinch of salt and pepper. Mix together until the grated ingredients are coated in the flour.

❸ Heat the sunflower oil in a frying pan over a medium heat. Meanwhile, shape the mix into small, flat patties. Test that the oil is hot enough by adding in a couple of strands of grated potato – they should gently sizzle.

❹ Carefully add the latkes to the pan and cook for 4–5 minutes on each side until golden. Do this in two batches if you need to, to avoid the latkes sticking together in the pan.

❺ Spoon the vegan cream cheese into a bowl and stir in the chives, reserving a few to scatter over at the end.

❻ Carefully remove the latkes from the pan and drain on kitchen paper. Place onto serving plates and top with generous spoonfuls of the cream cheese mix. Scatter with the remaining chives and season with extra salt and pepper, if you like.

Fig, walnut and mint crostini with smoked houmous

Elegant yet easy-to-make, these crostini make a beautiful starter course for your Christmas dinner. They are also perfect for serving as canapés, hors d'oeuvres or sharing plates throughout the festive season. Smoked houmous contrasts the flavour of the figs, making them taste almost sweeter and jammier. Lightly oven-toasted walnuts are crispy and add bitterness, while mint adds freshness and fragrance. Serve warm or cold.

Serves 4

1 small, day-old white baguette (French stick), sliced on the diagonal into 8 x 2cm (¾in) slices
2 tbsp good-quality extra virgin olive oil, plus extra for drizzling
6 shelled walnuts, roughly broken
1 garlic clove, halved
4 tbsp smoked houmous
4 ripe figs at room temperature, halved
8 mint leaves, roughly torn
generous pinch of sea salt

1 Preheat the oven to 190°C/375°F/gas mark 5.

2 Arrange the slices of bread on a large baking tray, and use a pastry brush to brush both sides of the bread with the 2 tablespoons olive oil. Bake in the oven for 8–10 minutes until lightly golden and crisp.

3 Meanwhile, arrange the walnuts on a smaller baking tray and toast in the oven for 4–5 minutes. Remove from the oven at set aside.

4 Remove the crostini from the oven and allow to cool for a couple of minutes. Rub the cut sides of garlic clove over the tops to press in extra flavour.

5 Smooth the houmous evenly over each crostini, about ½ tablespoon per slice.

6 Gently squeeze each fig half to loosen the jammy centre, then place one half on each crostini. Press on the toasted walnut pieces, then scatter over the mint leaves and season with a pinch of sea salt. Finally drizzle with a little olive oil.

Easy tip

Smoked houmous is readily available in supermarkets, and brings depth of flavour with minimal effort. Not only is it delicious in this recipe, but it's also versatile to be used as a dip for crudités, or spooned onto flatbreads with grilled aubergines (eggplants).

Mini no-fish bites with yogurt caper dip

These elegant mini no-fish bites have a crisp golden outer, and a fluffy potato and herb centre. Canned jackfruit, which you can now find in most supermarkets, gives the texture of flaked fish, with a mild flavour to let the herbs sing! Serve as a sharing platter, or as individual-sized portions with a leafy side salad and plenty of the tangy yogurt, for dipping.

Serves 4

4 large baking potatoes, peeled and roughly chopped

1 x 400g (14oz) can of jackfruit, drained and rinsed

4 tbsp vegan mayonnaise

30g (1oz) pack of fresh chives, finely chopped

generous handful of fresh dill, finely chopped

small handful of flat-leaf parsley, finely chopped

generous pinch of sea salt and black pepper

4 tbsp sunflower oil

For the yogurt caper dip

4 rounded tbsp unsweetened soya yogurt

2 tbsp capers in brine, drained

pinch of black pepper

squeeze of juice from an unwaxed lemon, with wedges to serve

❶ Bring a large pan of water to the boil over a medium-high heat, add the potatoes and boil for 20–25 minutes until tender. Thoroughly drain away the water, then mash the potatoes until smooth. Allow the mashed potato to cool until it is comfortable enough to handle.

❷ After draining and rinsing the jackfruit, place it on kitchen paper or a clean tea towel to drain off any remaining liquid. Add the jackfruit to a bowl, separating the chunks into strands.

❸ Add the mashed potato to the bowl and stir in the mayonnaise, chives, dill and parsley. Season generously with sea salt and black pepper, then stir to combine.

❹ Spoon 2 rounded teaspoons of the mixture into your hands and shape into a flat patty. Repeat until all of the mixture has been used. Place the patties on a plate, then refrigerate overnight, or for at least 4 hours.

❺ Remove the patties from the fridge and heat the oil in a frying pan over a medium-high heat. When the oil is hot, place a few patties into the pan and cook on each side for 4–5 minutes until golden and crisp. Cooking the no-fish bites in batches will make it easier to flip each one in the pan.

❻ To make the yogurt caper dip, stir together the yogurt, capers, black pepper and lemon juice. Spoon into individual ramekins, or one small serving bowl.

❼ Serve the hot no-fish bites with wedges of lemon and the yogurt dip.

Easy tip

For the best texture, refrigerate the mixture overnight, or for at least 4 hours. This also helps the mixture stay firm in the pan, making the no-fish bites easier to flip and cook evenly.

Sage, onion and chestnut rolls

Crisp, golden and packed with all the flavours of Christmas, these bite-sized treats will be a hit with everyone. Serve hot or cold, with extra cranberry sauce for dipping.

Makes about 10 mini rolls

1 tbsp sunflower oil, plus 2 tsp for
  brushing
1 small onion, diced
1 tsp dried sage
180g (6oz) vacuum-packed roasted
  chestnuts, finely chopped
4 sheets of filo (phyllo) pastry
  (ensure vegan)
4 tsp cranberry sauce
½ tsp nigella seeds
generous pinch each of sea salt and
  black pepper

Easy tip

Shop-bought filo pastry is often dairy-free, but always check the ingredients before you buy. Take the filo pastry out of the pack sheet by sheet as you need it, as it tends to dry out quickly.

❶ Preheat the oven to 200°C/400°F/gas mark 6 and line two baking trays with greaseproof paper.

❷ Heat the 1 tablespoon sunflower oil in a large pan, then add the onion and dried sage. Cook for 2–3 minutes, stirring frequently, until the onion starts to soften.

❸ Add the chopped chestnuts, then cook for another 2 minutes. Season with salt and pepper, then remove from the heat.

❹ Lay out one sheet of the filo pastry on a clean, flat surface. Use a pastry brush to sweep over a little sunflower oil, then place a second sheet of filo pastry on top of the first.

❺ Spoon 2 teaspoons of the cranberry sauce in a straight line 4cm (1½in) from the top of the pastry. Spoon half of the chestnut mixture over the cranberry sauce. Roll the pastry to form a log shape, rolling tightly to secure the filling.

❻ Use a sharp knife to cut the roll into 5 even pieces, then place on a baking tray. Brush the tops with a little sunflower oil, then scatter over half the nigella seeds. Repeat with the remaining pastry, filling and seeds.

❼ Bake in the oven for 25 minutes until golden and crisp.

Mushroom, garlic and thyme pâté with paprika

It wouldn't be Christmas without a thick, savoury pâté ready to be spread liberally on melba toast (or any toast). This pâté is equally delicious on crackers, as a dip for crudités, or on an open sandwich. Serve with a handful of small, pickled gherkins on the side, if you like.

Serves 4

1 tbsp sunflower oil

250g (9oz) chestnut (cremini) mushrooms, wiped clean and roughly quartered

2 sprigs of thyme

generous pinch of sweet paprika

2 garlic cloves, crushed

150g (5oz) vegan cream cheese

handful of flat-leaf parsley, finely chopped

generous pinch each of sea salt and black pepper

Easy tip

For a coarser pâté, roughly blitz the mushroom mixture in a food processor, and then stir into the cream cheese. For a smoother pâté, blitz the mushrooms and cream cheese together in the food processor before chilling.

❶ Heat the oil in a pan over a medium heat, then throw in the mushrooms. Pull the thyme leaves from the stalks and stir through the mushrooms. Cook for 5–6 minutes until fragrant, stirring frequently.

❷ Stir in the paprika and garlic and cook for a further 2 minutes. Remove from the heat and season with salt and pepper.

❸ Spoon the mushroom mixture into a food processor and blitz until coarsely chopped. Scrape the mushroom mix into a bowl and fold in the vegan cream cheese. Stir until evenly distributed.

❹ Lightly stir in the chopped parsley, then spoon into ramekins or a small food storage container. Chill for at least 4 hours, or overnight.

Pumpkin seed and black pepper crackers

Impress your guests with these homemade crackers, perfect for loading with mushroom, garlic and thyme pâté (page 44), or for serving with soup as an alternative to bread. Also delicious with a vegan cheeseboard.

Serves 4

150g (1¼ cups) plain (all-purpose) flour

4 tbsp pumpkin seeds

¼ tsp cracked black pepper (about 6 turns on a pepper mill)

1 tsp sea salt, plus extra for finishing

½ tsp caster (superfine) sugar

2 tbsp olive oil

Easy tip

These crackers will keep for up to a week in a sealed container when stored in a cool place.

1 Preheat the oven to 200°C/400°F/gas mark 6.

2 Stir together the flour, pumpkin seeds, black pepper, sea salt and caster sugar in a bowl.

3 Make a well in the centre of the mixture, then spoon in the oil and 70ml (⅓ cup) cold water. Use your hands to bring everything together into a dough.

4 Tip the dough out onto a piece of baking parchment and use a rolling pin to roll the dough to a 5mm (¼in) thickness. Sprinkle with a generous pinch of sea salt and gently push the flakes into the dough, then use a sharp knife to slice the crackers into bite-sized squares.

5 Transfer the crackers, still on the sheet of baking parchment, to a baking tray. Bake in the oven for 12–15 minutes until lightly golden, then allow to cool for at least 10 minutes to crisp up.

Spiced parsnip soup with beetroot crisps

Roasted parsnips have a comforting sweetness, especially when combined with gentle spices and coconut milk in this family-friendly soup. Switch croutons for slow-baked beetroot crisps, for a pop of colour and a perfect crisp crunch in your bowl. For the smoothest soup, blitz in a high-powered jug blender, or blitz for longer if using a stick blender.

Serves 4
The soup is suitable for freezing, but the beetroot crisps are best cooked fresh

500g (1lb 2oz) parsnips, peeled and
    roughly chopped
2 carrots, peeled and roughly chopped
1 onion, quartered
2 tbsp sunflower oil
2 tsp garam masala
pinch of dried chilli flakes
1 x 400ml (14fl oz) can of coconut milk
600ml (2½ cups) hot vegetable stock
generous pinch each of sea salt and
    black pepper
small handful of flat-leaf parsley,
    leaves only

For the beetroot crisps
1 beetroot (beet), peeled and very thinly
    sliced using a mandoline or sharp knife
drizzle of sunflower oil

Easy tip

The beetroot crisps can be made up to 2 days in advance and stored in an airtight container, preferably on kitchen paper, to avoid any moisture softening the crisps.

1 Preheat the oven to 150°C/300°F/gas mark 2 and line one large or two smaller roasting trays with baking parchment.

2 First make the beetroot crisps. Toss the beetroot slices into a bowl and stir through the oil to coat evenly. Place the beetroot slices on the lined roasting tray/s, arranged so they don't touch each other. Bake in the oven for 1 hour, turning the tray/s after 30 minutes so the crisps cook evenly. When the slices are crisp, remove the tray/s from the oven and allow to cool fully.

3 To make the spiced parsnip soup, place the parsnips, carrots and onion onto a roasting tray and drizzle with the sunflower oil. Roast in the oven for 30 minutes until golden and softened.

4 Remove the roasted vegetables from the oven, and spoon into a high-powered jug blender (or into a large pan if you are using a stick blender). Add the garam masala and chilli flakes, then pour in the coconut milk and hot vegetable stock. Blitz until completely smooth, then season to taste with salt and pepper.

5 Ladle into warmed bowls, then scatter with a few parsley leaves and some beetroot crisps before serving.

The
Main
Event

Jerusalem artichoke rosti with carrot purée, crispy cavolo nero and walnuts

This special dinner is set to impress. It is, in fact, very simple to prepare and put together. If you've ever wondered what to do with knobbly Jerusalem artichokes, this is a great way to enjoy them. Golden rosti are nestled on sweet, smooth carrot and nutmeg purée, then topped with crisp, just-bitter cavolo nero and walnuts. It can be prepared in advance in stages, for a stress-free Christmas dinner.

Serves 4

For the carrot purée

3 carrots, peeled and roughly chopped

generous pinch of freshly grated nutmeg

1 tsp vegan butter

1 tbsp vegan cream

pinch of sea salt and black pepper

For the rosti

400g (14oz) Jerusalem artichokes, peeled and grated

400g (14oz) baking potatoes (around 2 medium potatoes), peeled and grated

¼ brown onion, diced

2 tbsp sunflower oil

2 leaves of cavolo nero, roughly chopped, stem discarded

1 tbsp walnuts, roughly chopped

sea salt and black pepper

Easy tip

The rosti can be made up to 8 hours in advance. Simply drain them on kitchen paper and then reheat in the oven or microwave before serving.

1 To make the carrot purée, bring a pan of water to the boil, add the carrots and simmer for 20 minutes until tender. Drain away the water and add the carrots to a high-powered jug blender or food processor, along with the nutmeg and butter. Blitz until almost smooth, scraping the sides of the jug as needed, then add the cream and blitz until completely smooth. Season with salt and plenty of pepper and set aside.

2 Put the Jerusalem artichokes and potatoes into a clean, dry tea towel and squeeze over a sink to remove as much liquid as possible. Then lay out on kitchen paper or another clean, dry tea towel for a few minutes to soak up any excess liquid.

3 Add the grated Jerusalem artichokes and potatoes to a bowl and stir in the diced onion and a pinch each of salt and pepper.

4 Use your hands to make about 8 small, round rosti. (I like doing this by hand as it looks a little more rustic, and the edges become nice and crispy during cooking, but for a more uniform size and shape, press through a chef's metal ring, or scone cutter.)

5 Heat the oil in a frying pan over a medium-high heat. Add the rosti and cook for 6–8 minutes until golden and crisp, then carefully flip them over and cook for a further 6–8 minutes until golden. Remove from the pan and drain on kitchen paper, then keep them warm in a low oven.

6 Return the pan to the heat and increase the heat to high. Throw in the cavolo nero and walnuts and stir-fry for 4–5 minutes until crisp and toasted. Meanwhile, reheat the carrot purée, in a small pan or in the microwave.

7 Lay out your serving plates. Add a generous tablespoon of carrot purée to the plate, then run the back of your spoon through it. Lay over 2 rosti, then top with crispy cavolo nero and walnuts.

Buttery mushroom, chestnut and thyme wellington

Present this crowd-pleasing wellington at your Christmas dinner table and let your guests delight in seasonal flavours and golden, puff pastry. This is very simple to prepare with just a few staple ingredients, so you can feel confident that your wellington will be succulent and fail-safe for the big day. Many brands of shop-bought puff pastry are vegan friendly, but always check the ingredients before you buy. This is delicious served with lashings of ultimate vegan gravy (page 106) and a spoonful of bay-infused bread sauce (page 116) on the side.

Also pictured on page 9.

Serves 4 generously

1 tsp vegan butter

250g (9oz) chestnut (cremini) mushrooms, brushed clean, sliced into quarters

2 sprigs of fresh thyme, leaves stripped from the stems

3 garlic cloves, crushed

3 spring onions (scallions), finely chopped

180g (6oz) vacuum-packed cooked chestnuts, roughly chopped

400g (14oz) can white beans, rinsed, drained and blended

1 sheet of ready-rolled puff pastry (ensure vegan; see page 15)

1 tsp soya milk, to glaze

generous pinch each of sea salt and black pepper

Easy tip

Prepare the filling on Christmas Eve, and keep it refrigerated ready to cook in puff pastry on Christmas Day.

---

❶ Melt the vegan butter in a frying pan over a medium heat, then throw in the mushrooms and thyme leaves. Cook for 4–5 minutes, stirring occasionally.

❷ Add the garlic and spring onions and cook for a further 2 minutes until fragrant, then remove the pan from the heat and stir in the chopped chestnuts and blended beans. Season very well with salt and pepper, then allow to cool for a few minutes.

❸ Lay out a large sheet of cling film (plastic wrap). Spoon the mushroom mix into the centre of the cling film, then wrap it securely. Place in the fridge for at least 2 hours, or overnight.

❹ Preheat the oven to 200°C/400°F/ gas mark 6 and line a baking tray with baking parchment. Remove the puff pastry sheet from the fridge 10 minutes before using, so it is more pliable and less likely to crack.

❺ Unroll the pastry on a clean surface, with the shorter edge facing towards you. Remove the chilled mushroom mix from the fridge and place it in a line down the centre of the pastry, allowing it to spread to about 12–15cm (5–6in) wide. Wrap each longer side of the pastry inwards, pressing them together to seal.

❻ Carefully turn the pastry roll over, so the sealed edges are now underneath. Slice off the excess pastry at each side, then tuck the open edge under, pressing it in to seal. Reserve some of the excess pastry to cut out small festive shapes, such as stars or holly leaves, if you like.

❼ Place the wellington on the lined baking tray. Gently score the top of the wellington with a knife a few times in diagonal lines without cutting all the way through the pastry, or press on your pastry decorative shapes. Brush the top and sides with a little soya milk to glaze, then bake in the oven for 35–40 minutes until golden.

❽ Allow to rest for a few minutes before slicing into portions.

Smoky quiche with spinach, dill and lemon

Serve a slice of this elegant quiche as the star of your Christmas dinner. With its smoky, cheesy flavour, and fluffy filling, it is set to impress your guests. If you can't source smoked tofu, use regular extra-firm tofu and get the smoky flavour from smoked vegan cheese, which is now available in many large supermarkets. Or, if you really want to make a flavour impact, double up the smoky flavour with smoked tofu and smoked vegan cheese! Make as one whole quiche, then slice into portions, or bake in individual, mini quiche tins.

Serves 4

1 tsp vegan margarine, for greasing
1 sheet of ready rolled shortcrust pastry
  (ensure vegan)
1 tbsp sunflower oil
1 onion, diced
8 stalks of Tenderstem broccoli
  (broccolini), trimmed
2 generous handfuls of spinach leaves
280g (9oz) block of extra-firm
  smoked tofu
pinch of ground turmeric
3 tbsp vegan double (heavy) cream
100g (3½oz) hard vegan cheese, grated
handful of fresh dill, finely chopped
sea salt and black pepper
1 unwaxed lemon, cut into wedges

Easy tip

Allow the quiche to cool for a few minutes before slicing into portions, to enable the filling to firm up a little more for easy and clean slicing.

① Preheat the oven to 180°C/350°F/gas mark 4. Grease an 18cm (7in) quiche tin with vegan margarine, or line the base with baking parchment.

② Unroll the pastry over the quiche tin, pressing it down at the edges, then trim away the excess pastry.

③ Lay a piece of baking parchment over the pastry and add a handful of baking beans (pie weights), then blind bake in the oven for 10–12 minutes until lightly golden.

④ Meanwhile, heat the oil in a pan over a medium heat and add the onion. Cook for 2–3 minutes until the onion begins to soften, then add the broccoli and spinach. Cook for a further 2 minutes until the vegetables appear bright green (there's no need to cook any longer until softened, as they will be fully cooked in the oven later).

⑤ Blot the tofu on kitchen paper to remove any excess water, then break up into a few pieces and add to a high-powered jug blender or food processor. Add the turmeric and vegan cream, along with 3 tablespoons cold water. Blitz until a thick, smooth paste is formed, scraping the sides of the blender jug as you go. On the final blitz, add up to another 3 tablespoons cold water, to loosen the mix slightly, but it should not be watery; it should be thick enough to be spooned.

⑥ Stir in the cheese and most of the dill, reserving some to garnish, then season with a generous pinch of sea salt and black pepper.

⑦ Remove the pastry case from the oven and remove the baking parchment and baking beans. Spoon in half of the tofu mix, then scatter over the onions, broccoli and spinach. Smooth over the remaining tofu mix, stirring the mixture to bring some of the vegetables closer to the top, but ensuring they are coated in the mix to avoid burning.

⑧ Bake in the oven for 30–35 minutes until golden and set. Allow to cool for a few minutes before slicing, then sprinkle with the reserved dill. Serve with a wedge of lemon for squeezing.

Savoury roasted pears with red onions, sour cherries and pine nuts

If you've never roasted pears before, then you're in for a real treat – they are succulent, tender and delicious when cooked with woody herbs and red onions. Sour cherries offer a pop of colour and tartness, but if you don't have any available, fresh blackberries make a great alternative. Serve with caramelized onion gravy (page 108).

Serves 4

2 red onions, sliced into rounds

2 tbsp dried sour (tart) cherries

2 sprigs of fresh rosemary

4 large conference pears, halved, stalks and pips discarded

drizzle of sunflower oil

generous pinch of dried sage

1 tbsp pine nuts

generous pinch each of sea salt and black pepper

① Preheat the oven to 200°C/400°F/gas mark 6.

② In a deep baking dish, arrange the onions and sour cherries, then lay over the rosemary sprigs. Place the pear halves over the top, with the skin facing up. Drizzle with a little sunflower oil, then scatter the sage over the pears.

③ Roast in the oven for 30 minutes, then carefully scatter over the pine nuts and cook for a further 5–6 minutes until golden and toasted.

④ Remove from the oven and season with salt and pepper. Serve 2 halves of pear per person, along with plenty of the roasted onions and cherries.

Easy tip

I love the simplicity of this dish – and when served with all of the trimmings, it is filling and satisfying. If you wanted to add a little extra something, or stretch the recipe out further, pour in a 400g (14oz) can of drained and rinsed cannellini beans around the pears when you scatter over the pine nuts.

Follow the star shepherd's pie

This family favourite shepherd's pie is a real crowd pleaser – and a fail-safe option to make ahead. Rest assured that this recipe will be loved by both children and adults, with its familiar, homely flavours and festive star topping. The pie can be made in advance and then frozen for up to 3 months. Fully defrost and thoroughly reheat before serving.

Serves 4
Suitable for freezing

1 tbsp sunflower oil

1 onion, diced

2 carrots, peeled and sliced into
    half rounds

2 celery sticks, diced

1 garlic clove, crushed

generous glug of red wine (ensure vegan)

2 bay leaves

2 sprigs of fresh rosemary

1 sprig of fresh thyme

1 x 400g (14oz) can of green lentils,
    drained and rinsed

1 x 400g (14oz) can of chopped tomatoes

200ml (generous ¾ cup) hot vegetable
    stock

700g (1½lb) Maris Piper potatoes (around
    4 large potatoes), peeled and chopped

2 rounded tbsp vegan butter

1 tbsp vegan double (heavy) cream

generous splash of vegan Worcestershire
    sauce (ensure vegan as may contain
    anchovies)

sea salt and black pepper

> **Easy tip**
> You'll find large star nozzles (tips)
> available at cake decorating retailers.
> I'd recommend using a good-quality
> metal tip for the best shape and
> longevity.

1 Heat the oil in a large pan over a medium heat and add the onion. Cook for 2–3 minutes, then add the carrots and celery. Cook for a further 2–3 minutes until they begin to soften. Stir in the garlic and cook for another minute until fragrant.

2 Pour in the generous glug of red wine, along with the bay leaves, rosemary and thyme. Reduce for 5 minutes, stirring occasionally.

3 Stir in the green lentils, chopped tomatoes and vegetable stock, then reduce the heat to low-medium. Simmer for 30 minutes, stirring occasionally to prevent sticking.

4 Meanwhile, bring a large pan of water to the boil and add the potatoes. Cook for 20–25 minutes until fork-soft. Thoroughly drain away all of the water.

5 Add the butter and cream to the potatoes and mash until smooth and stiff. Bear in mind that this mashed potato will be pushed through a piping nozzle, so ensure it has no lumps. Don't be tempted to add any more cream, as it needs to be stiff enough to create the star shapes. Allow to cool.

6 Prepare a piping bag with a large star-shaped nozzle. When the mashed potato is cool enough to handle, spoon it into the piping bag.

7 Remove the bay leaves and tough stems of rosemary and thyme from the lentil mix. Season to taste with vegan Worcestershire sauce and a pinch of salt and black pepper.

8 Pour the lentil mix into an ovenproof dish. Allow it to cool for a few moments while you preheat the oven to 180°C/ 350°F/gas mark 4.

9 Pipe the mashed potato on top of the lentils. Work in lines, with short, sharp squeezes of the bag to get clean star shapes. Once the top is completely filled with mashed potato stars, bake in the oven for 35–40 minutes until the topping is golden and crisp at the peaks.

Brown sugar and spice tofu with split pea purée

Tender tofu is marinated in a sticky, spiced sauce before being cooked until just crisp, then served over a smooth pea purée infused with orange and coriander. This full-of-flavour dish is delicious throughout winter, but extra special when served on Christmas day.

Serves 4

100ml (scant ½ cup) light soy sauce

2 tbsp brown sugar

1 tbsp maple syrup

2 garlic cloves, crushed

1cm (½in) piece of ginger, peeled and finely chopped

pinch of chilli flakes

280g (9oz) block of pre-pressed extra-firm tofu, sliced horizontally into 4 'steaks'

100g (½ cup) dried yellow split peas, rinsed clean

zest and juice of 1 unwaxed orange

handful of fresh coriander (cilantro), finely chopped

1 tbsp sunflower oil

Easy tip

Pre-pressed extra-firm tofu is available in supermarkets and saves you the time and effort of pressing the tofu over a number of hours.

1 In a bowl, whisk together the soy sauce, brown sugar, maple syrup, garlic, ginger and chilli flakes.

2 Score the slices of tofu diagonally using a sharp knife. Place the slices of tofu into a large dish, then pour over all of the soy sauce mix. Ensure all of the tofu is coated, then allow to stand for an hour at room temperature to marinate.

3 Meanwhile, prepare the split pea purée. Add the split peas to a pan and cover with water. Bring to the boil for 10 minutes, then reduce the heat and allow to simmer for 30–35 minutes until softened.

4 Drain away the water and tip the cooked split peas into a high-powered jug blender or food processor. Add the orange zest and juice and blitz, adding in a couple of tablespoons of cold water to loosen further, if needed, to form a smooth purée. Stir in the fresh coriander.

5 Heat the sunflower oil in a large frying pan over a high heat. Add the tofu to the pan, then cook for 5–6 minutes on each side until the edges have started to crisp.

6 Reheat the split pea purée in a pan or microwave if needed. Lay out your serving plates, and add a generous swirl of purée to each plate. Lay the tofu over the purée.

Christmas cobbler

Creamy, comforting and topped with soft, golden cobbles – this Christmas cobbler is a family favourite. Fresh fennel and thyme infuse the cream sauce, for a wintery dish that is perfect all season long. If you don't have a hob-to-oven dish, cook the filling in a pan before transferring to an ovenproof dish, then add the cobbles and bake until golden.

Serves 4

1 tbsp sunflower oil

1 large leek, thinly sliced

1 carrot, peeled and finely chopped into half rounds

1 celery stick, thinly sliced

1 small fennel bulb, thinly sliced

2 leaves of cavolo nero, roughly sliced, tough stem discarded

2 garlic cloves, crushed

2 sprigs of thyme, leaves only

500ml (2 cups) hot vegetable stock

120ml (½ cup) vegan double (heavy) cream

1 x 400g (14oz) can or jar of butterbeans (lima beans), drained and rinsed

1 bay leaf

generous pinch each of sea salt and black pepper

For the cobbles

300g (2½ cups) self-raising flour

1 tsp dried sage

pinch of black pepper

100g (scant ½ cup) cold vegan butter

120ml (½ cup) unsweetened soya milk

Easy tip

The cobbles can be made up to a day in advance. Roll the dough into balls, then cover with cling film (plastic wrap) and refrigerate until use.

1 Pour the oil into a large hob-to-oven dish, then add the leek, carrot, celery, fennel and cavolo nero and cook over a medium-high heat for 4–5 minutes until they begin to soften.

2 Add the garlic and thyme and cook for a further minute.

3 Pour in the hot stock, vegan cream and butterbeans and add the bay leaf. Simmer for 15–20 minutes, then remove and discard the bay leaf. Season with salt and plenty of pepper and set aside.

4 Meanwhile, prepare the cobbles. In a large bowl, stir together the flour, sage and black pepper. Rub in the vegan butter until the mixture resembles breadcrumbs. Gradually pour in the soya milk, bringing the mixture together to form a thick dough. Make 12 golf-ball-sized cobbles, rolling them in your hands until smooth, and set aside. Meanwhile, preheat the oven to 200°C/400°F/gas mark 6.

5 Place the cobbles over the top of the dish, with a small gap between each one as they will expand a little in the oven. Cook in the oven for 20–25 minutes until the cobbles are risen and golden.

Crispy gnocchi with creamy kale, white wine and mushrooms

Treat your guests to this unexpected, Italian-style dinner with crispy pan-fried gnocchi and a creamy white wine and parsley sauce. I love to serve it in mini cast-iron pans, alongside all of the traditional trimmings, but it has also become a regular Christmas Eve supper in my house (served by the bowlful) as it's simple, comforting and warming.

Serves 4

500g (1lb 2oz) shop-bought gnocchi
(ensure vegan)

2 tbsp olive oil

250g (9oz) chestnut (cremini) mushrooms,
brushed clean and roughly sliced

2 handfuls of shredded kale, tough
stems discarded

2 garlic cloves, crushed

pinch of dried chilli flakes

glug of white wine (ensure vegan)

125ml (½ cup) vegan double (heavy)
cream

generous handful of flat-leaf parsley,
finely chopped

sea salt and black pepper

① Place the gnocchi into a large heatproof bowl and pour over enough boiling water to cover. Allow to stand for 2 minutes. Thoroughly drain away the water and pat the gnocchi dry using kitchen paper or a clean cloth.

② Add 1 tablespoon of the olive oil to a large frying pan and add the gnocchi, ensuring they are in a single layer. Cook over a medium-high heat for about 5 minutes without turning, then when they appear golden and crisp underneath, turn them over and cook the other side for a further 5 minutes until golden. Once crisp, tip the gnocchi onto a plate and set aside.

③ Return the pan to the heat and add the remaining tablespoon of olive oil. Add the mushrooms and cook for 5 minutes, stirring frequently. Throw in the kale and cook for a further 2–3 minutes. Stir in the garlic and chilli flakes and cook for a further minute, stirring constantly.

④ Pour in a glug of white wine and cook for 2 minutes, then stir in the vegan cream. Reduce the heat to medium and cook for 2–3 minutes, stirring frequently, until just bubbling.

⑤ Stir in the parsley, then season generously to taste with salt and plenty of pepper.

⑥ Return the gnocchi to the pan and lightly stir in (cooking it separately helps to keep the gnocchi crisp). Serve hot.

Easy tip

Gnocchi can be bought in most supermarkets, but always check the label, as it can sometimes contain eggs. The ambient varieties (rather than chilled) are more likely to be vegan. These packets will last for months in the cupboard, making them perfect to use in midweek suppers, or pan-fried until golden for special dinners.

Fennel seed sausages with chilli

These homemade sausages are a little bit special, with Italian flavours and a crisp skin. You can even serve them with Christmas ketchup (page 117) if you like. Alternatively, crisp up some strips of aubergine (eggplant) or vegan bacon in a pan, and wrap up the sausages – pigs in blankets style!

Makes 8
Suitable for freezing

2 tbsp sunflower oil, plus extra
    for brushing
300g (10oz) chestnut (cremini)
    mushrooms, brushed clean and
    roughly chopped
1 tsp fennel seeds
½ tsp dried chilli flakes
2 garlic cloves, crushed
2 spring onions (scallions), finely chopped
handful of flat-leaf parsley, finely
    chopped
6 tbsp rolled oats
generous pinch of sea salt and
    black pepper
4 rice paper wraps

Easy tip

Rice paper wraps are crisp in the packaging, so need to be softened in warm water for no more than 5 seconds before using to make them pliable. They can be a little delicate to handle at first, so ensure your work surface is oiled to make rolling the sausages easier. Rice paper wraps can be found in the world aisle of supermarkets. They can be called Vietnamese spring roll wraps (but are not to be confused with the crispy wraps used to make Chinese-style spring rolls).

1 Heat 1 tablespoon of the sunflower oil in a large pan over a medium-high heat, then throw in the mushrooms and fennel seeds. Cook for 5–6 minutes until fragrant, then add the chilli flakes, garlic and spring onions and cook for a further 2–3 minutes, stirring frequently to avoid sticking. Remove from the heat and stir in the parsley. Set aside to cool for a few minutes.

2 Add the oats to a high-powered jug blender and blitz for a few seconds until they become finer. Add the cooked mushroom mix to the oats, along with some salt and plenty of black pepper, then blitz again until a thick, coarse mixture is created.

3 Fill a large bowl with warm (not hot) water. Brush a clean worksurface or board with a little sunflower oil, as well as a plate to hold the sausages before you cook them. Dip a rice paper wrap into the water for 3–5 seconds until it begins to soften. Remove from the water and place on the oiled worksurface or board. Use a knife to slice the rice paper wrap in half.

4 Spoon 1 tablespoon of the blitzed mushroom mixture onto the centre of each half, spreading it down the length in a sausage shape. Roll the sides of the wraps in, then fold or twist the ends in to make a sausage shape. Place on the oiled plate while you prepare the other sausages with the remaining softened rice paper wraps.

5 Heat the remaining tablespoon of sunflower oil in a pan over a low-medium heat. Add the sausages and cook for 10–12 minutes, turning only when crisp on the cooked side, until just golden.

Crispy bourguignon pie

Rich, classic and oh-so-wintery, this red-wine-infused pie has a filling of hearty mushroom bourguignon with a crisp, golden filo pastry topping. Many brands of shop-bought filo pastry use vegetable oil instead of dairy butter, making it accidentally vegan. Delicious with roasted garlic mash (page 88) and ten-minute maple and mustard greens (page 85).

Serves 4

2 tbsp sunflower oil

300g (10oz) chestnut (cremini) mushrooms, brushed clean and halved

pinch of smoked paprika

6 shallots, halved

2 carrots, peeled and thinly sliced into half rounds

2 garlic cloves, crushed

2 tsp plain (all-purpose) flour

300ml (1¼ cups) good-quality red wine (ensure vegan; see page 15)

200ml (generous ¾ cup) hot vegetable stock

1 tbsp tomato purée (paste)

2 sprigs of fresh thyme

1 sprig of fresh rosemary

2 bay leaves

6 sheets of shop-bought filo (phyllo) pastry (ensure vegan)

sea salt and black pepper

❶ Heat 1 tablespoon of the oil in a pan over a medium heat, then throw in the mushrooms and smoked paprika. Cook for 5 minutes until fragrant. Tip the mushrooms onto a plate and set aside.

❷ Return the pan to the heat and add the remaining tablespoon of oil. Add the shallots and carrots, and soften for 4–5 minutes. Add the garlic and cook for a further minute. Sprinkle in the flour and stir to coat all of the vegetables.

❸ Pour in the wine and stock, then stir in the tomato purée. Add the thyme, rosemary and bay leaves, then bring to the boil and simmer for 10–15 minutes until the sauce has thickened.

❹ Once the sauce has thickened, remove and discard the thyme, rosemary and bay leaves and allow the sauce to cool for a few minutes, then stir in the mushrooms. Season with a pinch of salt and pepper, then pour into a large pie dish and allow to cool further while you preheat the oven to 200°C/400°F/gas mark 6.

❺ Tear the filo pastry into strips, then scrunch them over the top of the bourguignon. These can be positioned randomly and roughly until the top is covered.

❻ Bake in the oven for 15–20 minutes until the topping is crisp and golden.

Easy tip

For an alternative with a smoky flavour, fry up some chunks of smoked tofu (from a 400g/14oz block) in place of the mushrooms.

Chestnut cassoulet with sage dumplings

This is one of my favourite Christmas recipes – it's comforting, double-cooked and topped with sage-flavoured dumplings. I love to cook this in a cast-iron casserole dish and serve from oven to table, so everyone can tuck in family-style.

Serves 4
Suitable for freezing

1 tbsp sunflower oil

1 onion, finely diced

2 celery sticks, diced

2 carrots, sliced into half rounds

2 large leaves of cavolo nero

2 garlic cloves, crushed

1 tsp dried sage

generous glug of red wine (ensure vegan)

1 x 400g (14oz) can of good-quality chopped tomatoes

400ml (generous 1½ cups) hot vegetable stock

1 tbsp tomato purée (paste)

2 x 200g (7oz) vacuum-packed roasted chestnuts

2 sprigs of fresh rosemary

1 bay leaf

sea salt and black pepper

For the dumplings
150g (1¼ cups) self-raising flour

70g (2½oz) vegetable suet

1 tsp dried sage

generous pinch of sea salt

Easy tip
The dumplings can be made up to a day in advance, and kept chilled and covered until use.

❶ In a large, lidded hob-to-oven casserole dish, heat the oil and onion over a medium heat for 2–3 minutes until the onion starts to soften. Add the celery, carrots and cavolo nero and cook for a further 2 minutes.

❷ Throw in the garlic and dried sage and cook for 1 minute until the garlic becomes fragrant, then pour in the red wine and reduce for 2–3 minutes.

❸ Stir in the chopped tomatoes, stock, tomato purée and chestnuts. Add the rosemary sprigs and bay leaf, then simmer for 20–25 minutes, stirring occasionally to avoid sticking, until the cassoulet has reduced slightly.

❹ Remove from the heat, then discard the sprigs of rosemary and the bay leaf. Season to taste with salt and pepper and allow to rest for a few minutes while you preheat the oven to 160°C/320°F/gas mark 3.

❺ To make the dumplings, sift the flour into a bowl, then stir in the suet, sage and sea salt. Add about 3 tablespoons of cold water and mix to form a firm dough. If you require extra water, add it in one tablespoon at a time to make the dough pliable but not overly sticky. Roll the dough into 8 evenly sized balls.

❻ Place the dumplings on top of the cassoulet and cover with the lid. Cook in the oven for 20 minutes, then carefully remove the lid and cook for a further 10–15 minutes until the dumplings are golden and fluffy.

Spiced aubergines with toasted almonds and salted lemon yogurt

This versatile dish is fantastic as a lighter main dish for your Christmas dinner – and it works really well as an easy sharing dish to enjoy on Christmas Eve. It is gently spiced with harissa, but feel free to add more to suit your tastes. I love to cook this in one large dish, but it can be baked in individual dishes, if you like.

Serves 4

2 aubergines (eggplants), thinly sliced lengthways

2 tbsp olive oil

1 red onion, diced

2 garlic cloves, crushed

1 x 400g (14oz) can of good-quality chopped tomatoes

1 rounded tsp harissa

6 pitted green olives, sliced into rounds

generous handful of flat-leaf parsley, finely chopped

2 rounded tbsp flaked (slivered) almonds

4 tbsp plain soya yogurt

squeeze of juice from an unwaxed lemon

sea salt

❶ Preheat the oven to 180°C/350°F/gas mark 4.

❷ Layer the aubergines in a large baking dish, then drizzle with 1 tablespoon of the olive oil. Bake in the oven for 30 minutes.

❸ Heat the remaining tablespoon of olive oil in a pan and add the onion. Cook over a medium heat for 2–3 minutes, then add the garlic and cook for a further minute.

❹ Add the chopped tomatoes and harissa, then simmer for 15 minutes. Remove from the heat and stir in the olives and parsley.

❺ Remove the aubergines from the oven and pour the tomato mix over them. Return the dish to the oven for 20 minutes, then after 20 minutes, scatter over the almonds and cook for a further 10–12 minutes until they are golden.

❻ In a small bowl, stir together the yogurt, lemon juice and a pinch of salt. Keep chilled.

❼ Remove the baked aubergines from the oven. Spoon over random dollops of the yogurt just before serving.

Easy tip

Delicious served with all of your favourite trimmings, or anytime in winter with slices of thick, crusty bread.

Candy-cane onion tart

If you're looking for a quick and easy main dish, then this tart will become your go-to Christmas recipe. The roasted onion topping is tender, mellow and sweet. It may leave you wondering why you've never considered onions as the star of the show in other recipes too!

Serves 4

1 sheet of ready-rolled puff pastry
    (ensure vegan; see page 15)
2 red onions, thinly sliced into about
    5–6 rounds
2 brown onions, thinly sliced into about
    5–6 rounds
drizzle of olive oil
1 tsp vegan butter
½ tsp wholegrain mustard
small handful of flat-leaf parsley,
    roughly chopped
sea salt and black pepper

Easy tip
Remove the puff pastry from the fridge 30 minutes before using it, to avoid it cracking.

1 Preheat the oven to 180°C/350°F/gas mark 4.

2 Line a roasting tray with baking parchment paper and unroll the pastry onto it. Score along the edges of the pastry, about 1cm (½in) from the edge, to form a border. Spread over half the mustard.

3 Arrange the sliced onions on top of the pastry (you can do this randomly, or in stripes like a candy cane) and drizzle with a little olive oil. Bake in the oven for 20–25 minutes until the onions have softened and the pastry is golden and puffed around the edges.

4 Remove the tart from the oven. Mix together the butter and remaining mustard until combined, then brush this over the onions using a pastry brush.

5 Season with salt and pepper, then scatter with parsley and serve.

Butterbean gratin with basil crust

Tender butterbeans are cooked with saucy tomatoes and salty olives – the perfect main dish to serve with roasted vegetables and potatoes. Bake with a simple basil, almond and lemon crust, either in one large dish, or four smaller dishes. This would make a great budget-friendly Christmas dinner but is just as delicious served as your Christmas Eve supper.

Serves 4

1 thick slice of day-old crusty white bread
1 tbsp flaked (slivered) almonds
30g (1oz) fresh basil, finely chopped
zest of ½ unwaxed lemon, finely grated
pinch of black pepper
1 tbsp olive oil
1 onion, chopped
2 garlic cloves, crushed
1 tsp dried oregano
generous glug of red wine (ensure vegan)
1 x 400g (14oz) can of good-quality
    chopped tomatoes
pinch of granulated sugar
2 x 400g (14oz) cans or jars of butterbeans
    (lima beans), drained and rinsed
100g (3½oz) pitted green olives, sliced
6 cherry tomatoes, sliced
squeeze of juice from an unwaxed lemon
4 handfuls of fresh spinach leaves,
    stalks discarded
sea salt and black pepper

Easy tip

The butterbean filling can be made in advance and frozen for up to 3 months. Thoroughly defrost, then layer with spinach and a freshly prepared basil crust.

❶ Tear up the slice of bread and place in a food processor or high-powered jug blender with the flaked almonds and blitz or pulse until you create breadcrumbs. Tip the mix into a large bowl and stir in the basil and lemon zest. Season with black pepper, then set aside.

❷ Heat the oil in a large pan over a medium-high heat, add the onion and cook for 3–4 minutes, then add the garlic and oregano. Cook for a further minute until fragrant, then pour in the red wine and cook down for 2–3 minutes.

❸ Pour in the chopped tomatoes, sugar, butterbeans, olives and cherry tomatoes, then reduce the heat and simmer for 20 minutes.

❹ Squeeze in the lemon juice and stir in a small pinch of salt (remember that olives are naturally salty) and plenty of pepper. Preheat the oven to 180°C/350°F/gas mark 4.

❺ Spoon a layer of the butterbean mix into a large dish, then top with a handful of spinach leaves. Repeat to create about four layers. Finish by spooning the breadcrumb mix generously over the top.

❻ Bake in the oven for 30–35 minutes until the crust is golden and the filling is bubbling at the corners.

Apricot, pistachio and pomegranate roasted squash

*This gluten-free dish has it all – from bold
flavours and colours to satisfying textures.
Don't waste the excess softened flesh that
you remove in the recipe; either mash it with
potatoes or mix into squash pancakes!
Serve one half per person with roasted harissa
sprouts with dukkah (page 93) and garlic
mashed potatoes (page 88).*

Serves 4

2 large butternut squash, scrubbed
    clean and cut in half lengthways,
    seeds removed and discarded

2 tsp olive oil

200g (7oz) dried apricots, roughly
    chopped

150g (1¼ cups) shelled pistachios,
    roughly chopped

80g (3oz) pack of pomegranate seeds,
    or the seeds of 1 whole pomegranate

250g (9oz) pouch of cooked Puy (French)
    lentils

generous handful of fresh mint,
    finely chopped

generous handful of flat-leaf parsley
    finely chopped

1 tsp harissa paste

squeeze of juice from an unwaxed lemon

pinch of sea salt

Easy tip

There's no need to peel the
butternut squash as the skin
becomes tender during cooking and
is deliciously edible; just make sure
it is scrubbed clean, and no sticky
labels are in place!

❶ Preheat the oven to 190°C/375°F/gas mark 5.

❷ Lay the butternut squash halves on one large or two smaller
roasting trays, cut side up. Brush with olive oil, then roast in
the oven for 30 minutes.

❸ Meanwhile, add the apricots, pistachios and half of the
pomegranate seeds to a large bowl. Add in the lentils, mint
and parsley, then stir to combine.

❹ Remove the roasted butternut squash halves from the oven
and allow to cool for a few minutes. Scoop out some of the
soft flesh, leaving a 3–4cm (1¼–1½in) border around the
edge of each one.

❺ Lightly brush the spaces with harissa, then spoon in the
apricot mix. Return to the oven for a further 20 minutes.

❻ Remove from the oven and squeeze over the lemon juice.
Sprinkle over the remaining pomegranate seeds, then finish
with a pinch of sea salt.

Sides

Roasted hasselback parsnips with apples

These parsnips have the ideal balance of crispy, roasted skin, and a tender texture within. Parsnips can often become dry and somewhat chewy when roasted, but slicing into the vegetable allows the hot air to circulate and the cooking oil to make its way right into the centre. Hasselback parsnips also look fabulous for the festive season! The sweet and distinctive flavour of apples becomes intensified when roasted, providing the perfect accompaniment to parsnips.

Serves 4

6 parsnips, peeled and halved lengthways
2 apples, sliced into rounds, pips and
     tough outer stalk discarded
1 tbsp sunflower oil
generous pinch of dried sage
sea salt and black pepper

Easy tip

Parsnips are easier to 'hasselback slice' than potatoes, due to their shape and softer texture. To avoid slicing all the way through, lay the handles of two wooden spoons either side of the parsnip, then slice until the knife meets the handles.

---

❶ Preheat the oven to 180°C/350°F/gas mark 5.

❷ Lay one half of a parsnip on a flat surface and use a sharp knife to score into the parsnip, without slicing all of the way through, leaving 2mm between each score. Repeat for all of the parsnips.

❸ Place the hasselback parsnips onto a large roasting tray, leaving some space between each one. Lay in the apple slices.

❹ Brush the sunflower oil over the parsnips and apples using a pastry brush, then drizzle the excess into the roasting tray. Sprinkle over the pinch of dried sage.

❺ Roast in the oven for 45–50 minutes until the parsnips are golden brown and softened. Season with a pinch of salt and pepper. Serve hot.

Steamed Tenderstem broccoli with five-spice butter

Bring some vibrancy to your Christmas dinner table with this gently eastern-spiced broccoli, which the whole family will love. Chinese five-spice is a pre-mixed blend of selected spices, usually including cloves, star anise, fennel seed, cinnamon and Sichuan pepper, and is available in most supermarkets. It is a great addition to your store cupboard to add to other dishes, including rice and stir-fries, for year-round warming flavours.

Serves 4

200g (7oz) Tenderstem broccoli, tough stalk ends removed and discarded
2 tsp vegan butter, at room temperature
generous pinch of Chinese five-spice
pinch of sea salt
squeeze of juice from an unwaxed lime

Easy tip

The five-spice butter can be made up to 4 days in advance, then kept refrigerated in a sealed container or wrapped in cling film (plastic wrap). Soften at room temperature before use.

1 Bring a pan of water to the boil over a high heat. Place the broccoli in a steaming pan, and position over the boiling water. Steam for 4–5 minutes until just softened.

2 Meanwhile, in a small bowl, mix together the butter, Chinese five-spice and sea salt until combined.

3 Place the steamed broccoli into a warmed serving bowl, and stir through the spiced butter until melted and evenly distributed. Squeeze over the lime juice just before serving.

Ten-minute maple and mustard greens

Cook up this balanced and fresh side dish in under 10 minutes, and serve in a sharing bowl for everyone to help themselves. Prepare the vegetables in advance, then simply throw into the steaming pan as needed.

Serves 4 generously

2 leeks, finely chopped

½ savoy cabbage, roughly shredded

200g (7oz) green beans, ends trimmed

200g (7oz) Tenderstem broccoli

2 tbsp frozen peas

1 tsp maple syrup

1 tsp wholegrain mustard

4 tbsp good-quality extra virgin olive oil

sea salt and black pepper

Easy tip

Steam the green vegetables using a traditional steaming pan (over a pan of hot water), or an electric steamer.

❶ Bring a pan of water to the boil over a high heat and place the steaming pan over it. Allow the steaming pan to heat through.

❷ Throw in the leeks and cabbage and cook for 4 minutes, then throw in the green beans and broccoli and cook for 3 minutes. Scatter in the peas and cook for a further 2 minutes.

❸ Meanwhile, in a mixing bowl, whisk together the maple syrup, mustard, olive oil and a pinch of black pepper.

❹ Spoon the cooked vegetables into a serving bowl and toss in the oil until evenly coated. Season with sea salt to taste.

Ultimate roast potatoes

Christmas day is not complete without mountains of roast potatoes: golden and crispy on the outside, fluffy and piping hot in the centre. You've probably read (and tested) plenty of recipes for roast potatoes, but I always go back to the simplest method, one that works every time. The star of the show!

Serves 4

1.5kg (3lb 5oz) Maris Piper potatoes, peeled and chopped into large pieces
4 generous tbsp sunflower oil
flaky sea salt

Easy tip

Find my comprehensive guide to cooking the ultimate roast potatoes (with fail-safe tips) on page 16.

1 Bring a large pan of salted water to the boil over a high heat, then throw in the potato chunks. Boil for 10–15 minutes until just tender, then thoroughly drain away the water.

2 With the potatoes in the dry pan, cover with a lid and vigorously shake the pan to ruffle the outers of the potatoes.

3 Lay a clean tea towel out on the worktop, then place the potatoes on it. Cover with another clean tea towel and allow to stand overnight (in a cool place, or the fridge), or for at least 30 minutes.

4 Preheat the oven to 200°C/400°F/gas mark 6. Drizzle the sunflower oil into a deep roasting tray. When the oven has reached temperature, place the roasting tray in the oven for 10 minutes until the oil is glistening.

5 Remove the roasting tray from the oven, and use tongs to place the potatoes into the hot oil, turning to coat. Allow some room between each potato if possible.

6 Carefully return the roasting tray to the oven for 30 minutes, then turn the potatoes and return to the oven for a further 30 minutes until golden.

7 Remove from the oven and season with a generous pinch of flaky sea salt.

Roasted garlic mashed potatoes

Fluffy, moreish and oh-so-garlicky, these mashed potatoes are a real crowd-pleaser. The roasted garlic can be prepared up to a day in advance – don't be afraid to use the whole bulb, as the roasting process mellows the flavour. This freezes really well for up to a month, so this can be prepared in advance and frozen, then defrosted and thoroughly reheated on Christmas Day. The perfect time (and effort) saver!

Pictured on page 70.

Serves 4
Suitable for freezing

1 whole bulb of garlic, papery outer
    layer removed
drizzle of sunflower oil
1kg (2lb 4oz) Maris Piper potatoes,
    peeled and evenly chopped
3 tbsp vegan double (heavy) cream
2 rounded tbsp vegan butter
small handful of fresh chives,
    finely chopped
generous pinch of sea salt

Easy tip
Vegan double cream is available in most supermarkets, but can also be substituted for an unsweetened plant-based milk, or a generous spoonful of vegan cream cheese.

❶ Preheat the oven to 190°C/375°F/gas mark 5.

❷ Place the whole garlic bulb into a piece of foil and drizzle with sunflower oil. Scrunch up the kitchen foil to seal, then roast in the oven for 30–35 minutes until tender. Remove from the oven and carefully open the foil. Set aside until the garlic bulb is cool enough to handle.

❸ Meanwhile, bring a large pan of salted water to the boil over a medium-high heat, then add the potatoes. Boil for 15–20 minutes until tender, then remove from the heat.

❹ Thoroughly drain away the water, then allow the potatoes to stand for 2–3 minutes to steam dry (this will ensure the fluffiest mashed potatoes).

❺ Add the vegan cream and butter. Squeeze in the softened garlic from the bulb, discarding the outer layer.

❻ Use a potato masher to combine and mash the mixture until your desired consistency is reached. Don't forget to scoop potatoes from the outside of the pan into the centre to avoid large lumps.

❼ Return the pan to a low-medium heat for a couple of minutes. Once hot, stir in the chives and season to taste with sea salt.

Cacio e pepe cauliflower

Meet the simple and elegant sister of cauliflower cheese: cacio e pepe cauliflower. Vegan cheese and freshly cracked black pepper are stirred into a simple white sauce, before being baked over cauliflower. The white sauce is very simple to make, using store-cupboard ingredients; the trick to a good white sauce is to add the soya milk gradually, and whisk continuously until smooth. A fresh take on a familiar side dish, which was created to be shared.

Serves 4

1 cauliflower, broken into florets, leaves discarded
50g (scant ¼ cup) vegan butter
50g (1¾oz) plain (all-purpose) flour
500ml (2 cups) unsweetened soya milk
200g (7oz) hard vegan cheese (I prefer a cheddar-style)
sea salt and black pepper

Easy tip

The cheese and black pepper sauce is a great addition to any lasagne, and is also delicious baked over macaroni for a hearty winter supper.

❶ Bring a large pan of water to the boil over a medium-high heat, then add the cauliflower florets. Simmer for 5 minutes, then thoroughly drain away the water. Place the cauliflower into a deep-sided baking dish.

❷ Preheat the oven to 200°C/400°F/gas mark 6.

❸ Dry off the pan and return it to a low heat. Add the butter until just melted, then stir in the flour. Keep stirring until a thick paste (roux) is created. Cook for a further 2 minutes.

❹ Using a balloon whisk, gradually pour in the milk, whisking as you go. If the mixture appears to separate or split, whisk until it comes together before adding in any more milk. Once all of the milk is added, whisk continuously for 5–6 minutes, keeping the pan on the heat until it becomes a thick, smooth sauce.

❺ Remove from the heat and fold in half of the grated cheese, a pinch of salt and plenty of black pepper.

❻ Pour the sauce over the cauliflower, ensuring it is fully coated. Sprinkle the remaining grated cheese over the top, then bake in the oven for 25–30 minutes until golden and bubbling.

Pan-fried sprouts with butter, orange and lemon

I love pan-frying sprouts; it gets them crispy and caramelized on the outside, and perfectly tender through to the centre. The gentle bitterness of the charring is a match made in heaven with freshly grated lemon and orange zest and plenty of black pepper. Be sure to use a large frying pan, or two smaller frying pans, to allow the sprouts space to cook through. Smoked sea salt really lifts all of the flavours, but use regular flaked sea salt if that's what you have in the cupboard.

Serves 4

1 tbsp olive oil

300g (10oz) Brussels sprouts, tough stems trimmed, halved

1 tbsp vegan butter

zest and juice of 1 unwaxed lemon

zest of 1 unwaxed orange

generous pinch each of smoked sea salt and black pepper

Easy tip

Sprouts will last for longer when kept on the stalk, but if you've purchased a bag of sprouts, keep them in the fridge until ready to use for the best freshness and flavour.

1 Heat the oil in a large frying pan over a medium-high heat, then carefully add the sprouts, cut side down.

2 Fry for 7–8 minutes, tossing the pan occasionally to prevent sticking and burning, until golden and slightly charred.

3 Flip the sprouts and add the butter to the pan. Cook for a further 3–5 minutes until the butter has melted and the sprouts are fork-tender. Stir in the lemon zest and juice and the orange zest, then cook for a further minute, coating the sprouts in the citrus-butter mix.

4 Season to taste with smoked sea salt and plenty of black pepper. Serve hot.

Roasted harissa sprouts with dukkah

Add some serious flavour and spice to your Christmas dinner table with these harissa-roasted sprouts, with a crunchy and aromatic dukkah topping. Even the most dedicated sprout-hater will love this twist!

Serves 4

300g (10oz) Brussels sprouts, tough stems trimmed, halved

1 generous tbsp olive oil

2 rounded tbsp harissa

For the dukkah

50g (⅓ cup) blanched hazelnuts

3 tbsp sesame seeds

2 tsp cumin seeds

2 tsp fennel seeds

2 tsp coriander seeds

generous pinch of sea salt

Easy tip

Dukkah is a spice and nut blend, popular in the Middle East. It is easy to make, and will keep for up to 8 weeks in a sealed container or, if you'd prefer to use a shop-bought version, it is available in most large supermarkets.

❶ To make the dukkah, preheat the oven to 180°C/350°F/gas mark 4. Place the hazelnuts, sesame seeds, cumin seeds, fennel seeds and coriander seeds onto a roasting tray, then roast for 8–10 minutes until golden and there is a toasted fragrance.

❷ Remove the tray from the oven and spoon into a food processor. Pulse until everything is finely chopped, but not smooth. Stir in the sea salt, then set aside.

❸ Increase the oven temperature to 200°C/400°F/gas mark 6 ready for roasting the sprouts. Lay the spouts onto one large (or two smaller) roasting trays, with half cut side down, and half cut side up.

❹ Combine the oil and harissa in a small bowl. Use a pastry brush to liberally brush the mix over the sprouts, then drizzle any remaining over the top.

❺ Roast in the oven for 25–30 minutes until the sprouts are tender and caramelized. Remove from the oven and scatter generously with dukkah before serving the sprouts hot.

Winter gratin with sage cream

*A root vegetable gratin is the perfect addition
to your Christmas dinner table, combining
many seasonal vegetables in a satisfying side
dish. I've also been known to enjoy the leftovers
with a few salad leaves the next day. Feel free
to sprinkle over some grated vegan cheese for
the final bake, if you like.*

Serves 4
Suitable for freezing

2 tbsp sunflower oil
2 baking potatoes, peeled and thinly
    sliced into rounds
½ butternut squash, peeled and sliced
4 carrots, peeled and thinly sliced
1 sweet potato, peeled and thinly sliced
    into rounds
1 garlic clove, crushed
1 tsp dried sage
250ml (1 cup) soya single (light) cream
generous pinch each of sea salt and
    black pepper

> ### Easy tip
> This dish can be cooked a day in
> advance, kept in the fridge, and then
> reheated in the oven until piping
> hot. Simply sprinkle the top with a
> few drops of water before reheating
> to avoid it drying out.

❶ Preheat the oven to 200°C/400°F/gas mark 6.

❷ Spoon 1 tablespoon of the sunflower oil into a small bowl
ready for brushing the vegetables. In a gratin dish or deep
baking tray, arrange a layer of potato slices, and brush with
a little oil. Lay over the butternut squash and brush with oil,
then add a layer of carrot slices and brush with oil, followed
by the sweet potato slices brushed with oil. Cover the dish
loosely with foil, then bake in the oven for 30 minutes.

❸ Meanwhile, heat the remaining sunflower oil in a pan over
a low-medium heat and cook the garlic and sage until
softened and fragrant, about 12 minutes. Pour in the soya
cream and stir until combined with the garlic and sage.
Season to taste with salt, then remove from the heat.

❹ Carefully remove the gratin dish from the oven and discard
the foil. Pour over the cream mixture, then return the dish
to the oven for 30–35 minutes until the top is golden.

❺ Season with black pepper and serve hot.

All-in-one whole roasted vegetables

If you're looking for an easy side dish, then look no further than this all-in-one tray of chunky roasted vegetables. With no need for parboiling, and very little chopping involved, this is a fuss-free alternative to cooking and serving side dishes separately. Finish with a knob of vegan butter to melt over, if you like.

Serves 4

4 carrots, peeled, ends trimmed

4 parsnips, peeled, ends trimmed

2 large red onions, halved

2 fennel bulbs, halved

1 bulb of garlic, tough stem and papery
     outer layer removed

2 sprigs of fresh rosemary

2 sprigs of fresh thyme

generous drizzle of olive oil

generous pinch of sea salt

Easy tip

Roast up more vegetables than needed, so you can make Boxing Day Balti (page 129) with the leftovers.

1 Preheat the oven to 180°C/350°F/gas mark 4.

2 Arrange the carrots, parsnips, onions, fennel and garlic over one large, or two smaller, roasting trays, allowing a little space between each vegetable.

3 Lay over the rosemary and thyme sprigs, then drizzle the vegetables with a good drizzle of olive oil, about 3–4 tablespoons. Shake the tray (or trays) to distribute the oil.

4 Roast in the oven for 45–55 minutes, removing the tray/s from the oven when the vegetables are softened, golden and crisp at the edges (larger vegetables can take 55 minutes, but check at 45 minutes). Discard the herb stems and use a fork to squeeze the garlic from the bulb. Lightly toss, season to taste with sea salt and serve.

Sticky marmalade carrots

The humble carrot deserves a place at the Christmas dinner table. Its cheery orange hue lifts us all year round, it is a nutritional powerhouse, and it's a cheap and versatile vegetable. Show your carrots some love by roasting them in orange marmalade, for a caramelized, sticky glaze that will become a new Christmas tradition.

Serves 4

4 large carrots, peeled and halved
   lengthways
1 tbsp sunflower oil
1 rounded tbsp thick-cut orange
   marmalade
2 sprigs of fresh thyme
coarsely grated zest of ¼ unwaxed orange
generous pinch each of sea salt and
   black pepper

Easy tip

For a twist on this recipe, replace the thyme with a pinch of chilli flakes, then top with fresh coriander (cilantro) and a few drops of soy sauce just before serving.

---

1 Preheat the oven to 190°C/375°F/gas mark 5.

2 Arrange the carrots in a single line on a large roasting tray (or two smaller roasting trays). Brush the carrots with sunflower oil, then drizzle over any remaining oil. Roast in the oven for 25–30 minutes.

3 Carefully remove the hot tray from the oven. Generously spread the marmalade over the carrots to glaze. Pull the thyme leaves from the sprigs (discarding the tough stems) and scatter the leaves over the carrots.

4 Roast in the oven for a further 10–12 minutes until sticky and softened.

5 Remove from the oven and season with a pinch of sea salt and black pepper. Sprinkle with orange zest and serve hot.

Charred cabbage wedges with chilli, tomatoes and olives

Reimagine the humble cabbage! Roast wedges of cabbage until lightly charred, for extra flavour and an unexpected wow factor. Spoon over tomatoes, olives and parsley for an Italian twist that everyone will love.

Serves 4

1 savoy cabbage, cut into quarters, then each quarter halved again (8 wedges in total)

2 tbsp olive oil

generous pinch of chilli flakes

250g (9oz) cherry tomatoes, chilled, roughly diced

generous handful of flat-leaf parsley

100g (3½oz) pitted black olives, sliced into rounds

sea salt and black pepper

Easy tip

The tomato, olive and parsley 'salsa' can be made up to a day advance and kept in the fridge until ready to serve.

1 Preheat the oven to 200°C/400°F/gas mark 6.

2 Place the cabbage wedges on a large roasting tray (or two smaller roasting trays) and brush all over with olive oil. Sprinkle over the chilli flakes.

3 Roast in the oven for 15 minutes, then carefully turn over each wedge, and return to the oven for a further 15–20 minutes until softened and slightly charred in places.

4 Meanwhile, combine the tomatoes, parsley, black olives and a generous pinch of sea salt in a bowl.

5 Remove the wedges from the oven and place onto a serving plate. Season with black pepper, then spoon over the tomato mix and serve while the cabbage is hot.

Red cabbage with orange, cinnamon and black pepper

I love a generous helping of red cabbage with my Christmas dinner, especially this recipe which has a delicious balance of sweet and sour flavours, and plenty of aromatic spices.

Pictured on page 9.

Serves 4

1 red cabbage, finely shredded

1 apple, grated

200ml (generous ¾ cup) good-quality
    fresh orange juice

1 cinnamon stick

2 star anise

2 bay leaves

1 tbsp granulated sugar

1 tbsp apple cider vinegar

generous pinch of black pepper

1 Put the cabbage and apple into a large pan and pour in the orange juice.

2 Add the cinnamon, star anise, bay leaves and sugar, then bring to the boil over a high heat. Once boiling, reduce the heat to low-medium and allow to simmer for 30–35 minutes.

3 Remove from the heat and stir in the cider vinegar. Finish with a generous grind of black pepper. Serve hot.

Easy tip

Feel free to shred the cabbage in advance, but this dish is at its best when cooked fresh, just before serving.

Ciabatta, kale and sage stuffing

Chunky, rustic and oh-so-crispy, this stuffing is delicious sliced into (generous) pieces and served with your Christmas dinner. Earthy flavours of mushrooms and kale are delicious alongside the traditional sage and onion, in this twist on a classic.

Serves 6 generously

1 tbsp sunflower oil

1 onion, diced

6 chestnut (cremini) mushrooms, brushed clean and quartered

2 tsp dried sage

2 generous handfuls of shredded kale, stems removed

handful of flat-leaf parsley, torn

½ tsp vegan butter, for greasing

500g (1lb 2oz) loaf of day-old ciabatta, diced into bite-sized chunks

300ml (1¼ cups) hot vegetable stock

sea salt and black pepper

Easy tip

Day-old ciabatta really soaks up the flavours and helps the stuffing to 'set' in the roasting tray. If your ciabatta is very fresh and fluffy, bake it for 5–7 minutes at 100°C/210°F/gas mark ¼ to dry out a little.

1 Heat the sunflower oil in a large pan over a medium heat and add the onion, mushrooms and sage. Cook for 5–6 minutes until the onion starts to soften.

2 Add the kale, then cook for a further 2–3 minutes. Stir in the parsley and season with a generous pinch of salt and plenty of black pepper. Remove from the heat.

3 Preheat the oven to 180°C/350°F/gas mark 4 and grease a large roasting tray with vegan butter, to prevent the stuffing from sticking.

4 Stir the ciabatta chunks into the onion and mushrooms in the pan and lightly stir to combine. Pour in the stock and mix well, then press the ingredients from the pan into the roasting tray.

5 Cover the tray with foil and bake in the oven for 30 minutes, then remove the foil and cook for a further 20–25 minutes until the top is golden and crisp.

Pecan and green apple stuffing

Inspired by the festive flavours of the USA, this stuffing is so simple to make, and delicious to eat as part of your Christmas (or Thanksgiving) dinner and equally as wonderful served cold in a leftover sandwich! I often cook (and serve) this in a large lasagne tray for simple cooking, slicing and serving.

Serves 6
Suitable for freezing

1 tsp vegan butter, plus ¼ tsp for greasing
2 Granny Smith apples, cored and diced
150g (1 cup) pecans, roughly chopped
4 spring onions (scallions), finely chopped
1 tsp dried sage
¾ tsp ground cinnamon
3 slices of thick, day-old white bread
generous pinch of sea salt

Easy tip
There's no need to peel the apples; the skin gives extra texture to the stuffing and a hint of colour.

1 Melt the 1 teaspoon of butter in a pan over a low-medium heat, then add the diced apple and cook for 5–6 minutes. Add the pecans, spring onions, sage and cinnamon and cook for a further 5 minutes, then season with sea salt.

2 Preheat the oven to 180°C/350°F/gas mark 4. Grease a roasting tray with the ¼ teaspoon of butter.

3 Blitz the bread in a food processor or blender until it becomes fine breadcrumbs. Stir the breadcrumbs into the pan, then transfer the whole lot to the roasting tray, pressing it down as you go.

4 Bake in the oven for 30–35 minutes until golden and crisp on the top. Allow to cool for a few moments before slicing.

Gravy
& Sauces

Ultimate vegan gravy

Christmas dinner just wouldn't be the same without a rich, smooth gravy. Having tried and tested many recipes over the years, this is the one I always go back to, as it is excellent every time. The trick is to be patient at each stage – allow the mushrooms and vegetables to really brown over a high heat for plenty of flavour, then reduce the gravy until thick and smooth. And that teaspoon of coffee? It adds richness, depth and colour (and won't taste like your morning brew!).

Pictured on page 9.

Serves 4
Suitable for freezing

1 tbsp sunflower oil
6 mushrooms, brushed clean and
    roughly sliced
1 leek, sliced
1 carrot, peeled and sliced
1 celery stick, roughly sliced
3 sprigs of thyme
3 tsp plain (all-purpose) flour
700ml (2¾ cups) hot vegetable stock
1 bay leaf
1 tsp instant coffee granules
1 tbsp soy sauce
generous pinch of black pepper

Easy tip

The gravy can be made up to 3 months in advance and frozen, before being defrosted and reheated, or up to a day in advance when kept in the fridge.

❶ Add the oil and mushrooms to a large pan and cook over a high heat for 7–8 minutes. Stir the mushrooms frequently to allow browning. Some browning on the base of the pan is good for flavour, too.

❷ Add the leek, carrot, celery and thyme and continue to cook over a high heat for 8–10 minutes until they are softened and browned.

❸ Sprinkle in the flour and stir in to coat the vegetables. Cook for about a minute until the flour takes on the browned colour and no powdery patches are visible.

❹ Pour in the hot stock and stir everything vigorously, scraping any browned areas from the pan. Add the bay leaf and instant coffee, bring to the boil and cook for 12–15 minutes until the gravy has reduced to around 400ml (generous 1½ cups).

❺ Use a fork or potato masher to crush the softened vegetables to release extra flavour, then remove from the heat. Stir in the soy sauce.

❻ Place a sieve over a jug, then pour the gravy through the sieve. Press the vegetables again to release as much flavour as possible, then season the gravy to taste with black pepper. Pour into a warmed gravy jug to serve.

Caramelized onion gravy

If you're looking for an alternative to ultimate vegan gravy (page 106), this gravy is packed with flavour and the perfect balance of sweetness. It works well with pastry-based main courses, and of course with fennel seed sausages with chilli (page 67).

Serves 4
Suitable for freezing

2 tbsp sunflower oil
3 brown onions, thinly sliced
1 tsp soft light brown sugar
2 sprigs of thyme, leaves only
3 tsp plain (all-purpose) flour
700ml (2¾ cups) hot vegetable stock
2 bay leaves
1 tbsp balsamic vinegar
generous pinch of black pepper

1 Add the oil and onions to a large pan and caramelize the onions over a low-medium heat for 15–18 minutes, stirring often, until golden brown.

2 Stir in the sugar and thyme leaves, then cook for a further 4–5 minutes.

3 Sprinkle in the flour and stir to coat the onions. Cook for a further minute, stirring to avoid sticking.

4 Pour in the stock and add the bay leaves. Increase the heat to medium-high and cook for 12–15 minutes until thickened.

5 Stir in the balsamic vinegar and season to taste with black pepper. Remove the bay leaves before serving.

Easy tip

I like the slices of caramelized onion to remain in this gravy, for extra texture and flavour, but if you prefer your gravy without it, simply strain through a sieve into a jug or gravy boat.

Red wine sauce

A generous spoonful of rich red wine sauce is a real treat. The secret? Patience. If in doubt, leave the balsamic, wine and stock to reduce a little longer at each stage, for the smoothest, glossiest sauce. Serve with buttery mushroom, chestnut and thyme wellington (page 54).

Serves 4

1 tsp vegan butter
½ red onion, diced
1 garlic clove, crushed
1 tbsp good-quality balsamic vinegar
200ml good-quality red wine (ensure vegan; see page 15)
1 sprig of fresh rosemary
2 bay leaves
200ml (generous ¾ cup) hot vegetable stock
generous pinch of black pepper

Easy tip

Stir through a small handful of finely chopped flat-leaf parsley just before serving, for a variation on flavour and finish.

❶ Melt the vegan butter in a pan over a medium heat and add the red onion. Cook for 5–6 minutes until softened, then add the garlic and cook for a further minute.

❷ Pour in the balsamic vinegar and increase the heat to high. Cook for around 1 minute until it appears sticky and reduced.

❸ Pour in the wine, then add the rosemary sprig and bay leaves. Reduce for 5–6 minutes.

❹ Stir in the stock and bring to the boil, then simmer for 20–25 minutes until the sauce is reduced by around half and appears glossy and rich.

❺ Remove and discard the rosemary and bay leaves. Season to taste with black pepper.

Cranberry sauce with star anise and clementine

No Christmas dinner is complete without a generous spoonful of cranberry sauce. This simple and quick homemade version will knock the socks off any jarred version – who knew it was so easy? Perfect for gifting in festive hampers.

Serves 4 generously
Suitable for freezing

250g (9oz) fresh cranberries
juice of 3 clementines
2 rounded tbsp caster (superfine) sugar
1 star anise

Easy tip

This cranberry sauce can be cooked up to a month in advance and frozen, before being fully defrosted before use.

1 Put the cranberries into a pan and gently press them with a wooden spoon, to release their natural juices.

2 Add the clementine juice and stir in 2 tablespoons water.

3 Add the caster sugar and star anise, then simmer over a medium-high heat for 7–8 minutes, stirring occasionally to prevent sticking, until glossy and thick. Remove and discard the star anise.

4 Serve either warm or cold.

Balsamic red onion, blackberry and apple sauce

If cranberry sauce isn't your thing, try this tangy sauce, which tastes incredible with any roast vegetables. I love a spoonful with crispy gnocchi with creamy kale, white wine and mushrooms (page 66) or add a pot to your vegan cheeseboard.

Serves 4
Suitable for freezing

1 tbsp sunflower oil
1 red onion, thinly sliced
1 tbsp good-quality balsamic vinegar
150g (5oz) fresh blackberries
1 apple, grated
pinch of sea salt

Easy tip

This sauce isn't exclusive for Christmas dinner – switch your mango chutney for a spoonful of this tangy sauce.

1 Add the oil and onion to a pan and caramelize the onion over a medium heat for 10 minutes until softened and golden.

2 Add the balsamic vinegar and cook for a further 2 minutes.

3 Stir in the blackberries, breaking them down with a wooden spoon to release their natural juices, and the grated apple. Simmer for 10 minutes, stirring frequently to avoid sticking, until the blackberries have broken down.

4 Season with a small pinch of sea salt. Serve either warm or chilled.

Warm pomegranate, beetroot and mint relish

Earthy, sweet and fresh, this relish brings a lighter element to your dinner table. Delicious served with spiced aubergines with toasted almonds and salted lemon yogurt (page 72). Double up to serve as a vibrant sharing salad for a festive party.

Serves 4 generously

1 beetroot (beet), peeled and
    coarsely grated
seeds from 2 pomegranates
generous handful of fresh mint,
    finely chopped
small handful of flat-leaf parsley,
    finely chopped
zest and a squeeze of juice from
    1 unwaxed lemon
generous pinch of sea salt

❶ Add the beetroot, pomegranate seeds, mint, parsley and lemon zest to a pan, and warm over a low-medium heat for 3–5 minutes.

❷ Remove from the heat and squeeze in the lemon juice. Season to taste with sea salt. Serve warm.

Easy tip

If you want to avoid the task of removing pomegranate seeds, most supermarkets sell tubs of pomegranate seeds, to save you time, effort and mess!

Bay-infused bread sauce with nutmeg

Love it or hate it, bread sauce is a beige beauty, thought to have been popular since medieval times. This (vegan) milk and spice-infused sauce is thickened with bread. A British tradition not to be missed.

Pictured on page 55.

Serves 4
Suitable for freezing

1 onion, halved

5 cloves

3 bay leaves

1 tbsp black peppercorns

400ml (generous 1½ cups) unsweetened soya or oat milk

4 thick slices of day-old white bread, blitzed roughly into breadcrumbs

1 tbsp vegan butter

2 tbsp vegan cream

generous grating of fresh nutmeg

Easy tip

Tradition would have it that you should press the cloves into the onion, but I found that simply adding the onion and whole spices separately into the pan saves time, and is just as effective.

❶ Put the onion, cloves, bay leaves and peppercorns into a large pan, then pour in the milk. Bring to a simmer for 5 minutes over a low heat, then remove from the heat and allow to stand for an hour to infuse.

❷ Strain the milk through a sieve into another pan.

❸ Stir in the breadcrumbs, vegan butter and cream, then heat again over a low-medium heat for 5 minutes, stirring occasionally until thickened.

❹ Stir in the fresh nutmeg, reserving a little for sprinkling over the top to serve.

Christmas ketchup

There's always going to be that person who requests ketchup with their Christmas dinner (I see you). Serve them a festive treat with this seasonal-spiced edition! It's also delicious smoothed into a vegan sausage sandwich, all winter long.

Serves 6

1 tbsp sunflower oil
1 onion, diced
1 carrot, peeled and sliced
1 celery stick, peeled and sliced
2 garlic cloves, crushed
pinch of chilli flakes
2 tsp ground cinnamon
1 tsp allspice
½ tsp grated nutmeg
½ tsp ground cumin
2 tsp soft light brown sugar
500g (2 cups/17oz) good-quality passata (sieved tomatoes)
1 sprig of rosemary
generous pinch of sea salt

Easy tip

This ketchup will keep for up to 2 weeks when kept in the fridge in a sterilized, sealed jar.

❶ Heat the oil in a large pan over a medium heat, then add the onion, carrot and celery and cook for 5–6 minutes until softened, stirring frequently. Add the garlic and cook for a further minute.

❷ Stir in the chilli flakes, cinnamon, allspice, nutmeg and cumin and cook for another minute.

❸ Stir in the sugar, then pour in the passata. Add the rosemary, then reduce the pan to a low heat and simmer for 30 minutes, stirring occasionally.

❹ Remove the woody rosemary stalk and season the sauce with sea salt.

❺ Pour into a high-powered jug blender or food processor and blitz until completely smooth.

❻ Allow to cool fully, then pour into a sterilized jar or bottle. Keep refrigerated.

Cheat's no-cook Christmas chutney

Chutney and pickle can take hours – or even weeks – to prepare, but this no-cook chutney effectively prepares itself! The only effort required is to shake the jar each day (for 3 days) to infuse the apples and dried fruits. A delicious accompaniment to any vegan cheeseboard, or as a last-minute Christmas gift.

Serves 4

100ml (scant ½ cup) red wine vinegar
2 tsp soft light brown sugar
½ tsp ground cinnamon
½ tsp ground ginger
pinch of chilli flakes
pinch of grated nutmeg
2 red apples, peeled, cored and diced
1 tbsp dried cranberries
4 dried apricots, roughly diced

1 Add the vinegar, sugar, cinnamon, ginger, chilli flakes and nutmeg to a large, clean jar and shake to combine.

2 Add the diced apples, cranberries and apricots and shake to coat in the vinegar mix.

3 Place in the fridge for 3 days, shaking the jar each day to infuse the apples.

> **Easy tip**
> After the initial infusion period of 3 days, the chutney will then keep for another week in the fridge.

Brandy butter

Luxurious, rich and boozy, brandy butter is the perfect festive treat. Serve a generous spoonful with warm, vegan mince pies, or with the ten-minute figgy pudding (page 158).

Pictured on page 159.

Serves 4

100g (scant ½ cup) vegan butter
pinch of sea salt
½ tsp good-quality vanilla bean paste
75g (generous ½ cup) icing
    (confectioners') sugar
3 tbsp brandy (ensure vegan; see Easy Tip)

❶ In a large bowl, stir together the butter, sea salt and vanilla paste until combined.

❷ Roughly stir in the icing sugar, then use an electric whisk to beat until pale and fluffy.

❸ Whisk in the brandy, a tablespoon at a time, until combined. Chill for at least 1 hour before serving.

Easy tip

Some brands of brandy contain animal ingredients including eggs, fish and gelatine, which are used as processing agents. There are, however, many brands that are suitable for vegans so always check the label before you buy.

Leftovers

Bubble-and-squeak hash browns with avocado

The morning after the night before? These hash browns make the perfect brunch, topped with avocado and chilli. They also use up some of those veggies in the cupboard too.

Serves 4

1 large baking potato, grated

2 leaves of dark green cabbage, kale
    or cavolo nero, finely chopped

4 Brussels sprouts, finely sliced

½ small onion, diced

4 tbsp sunflower oil

2 avocados, peeled and sliced

few drops of Tabasco

small handful of fresh coriander
    (cilantro), roughly torn

generous pinch each of sea salt and
    black pepper

Easy tip

You don't need to peel the potato for these hash browns (it gives a rustic look and saves you the effort!) – simply scrub clean before use.

1 Grate the potato onto a clean, dry tea towel or cloth. Squeeze out as much moisture as possible into the sink. When no more liquid can be squeezed out, place the potato into a bowl.

2 Add the cabbage, sprouts and onion, then season with salt and pepper. Stir to combine all of the ingredients.

3 Taking 2 rounded tablespoons of the mixture at a time, shape the hash browns by firmly pressing together the mixture in your hands to form a flat round shape.

4 Heat the oil in a frying pan over a medium-high heat. Carefully add the hash browns and cook for 5–6 minutes on each side until golden and crisp.

5 Place the hash browns onto plates and top with half a sliced avocado per person. Sprinkle over a few drops of Tabasco, then top with coriander. Finish with a little extra sea salt, if you like.

Cheese and chutney bites

These crunchy, cheesy bites are the perfect accompaniment to a drink, or even as a light lunch. You can use a little more or less vegan cheese than the recommended amount, depending on what you have left in the fridge.

Makes 8

2 tsp sunflower oil
3 large tortilla wraps
8 tsp caramelized onion chutney
200g (7oz) hard vegan cheese (cheddar, smoked or mozzarella-style), grated
small handful of fresh chives, finely chopped
pinch of black pepper

Easy tip
I love using caramelized onion chutney in this recipe, but other chutneys such as fig or tomato work well too.

❶ Preheat the oven to 180°C/350°F/gas mark 4. Use a pastry brush to grease eight holes of a deep muffin tray with sunflower oil, then set aside.

❷ Lay out the tortilla wraps on a flat surface. Use a scone cutter (large enough to fill the muffin tray cup) to press out 16 circles.

❸ Press one single tortilla round into each muffin cup, then brush the surface with a little oil. Press on another tortilla round to make a double layer, making eight in total.

❹ Spoon 1 teaspoon of chutney into each tortilla 'cup', then sprinkle in the cheese.

❺ Bake in the oven for 8–10 minutes until the cheese has melted and the tortillas are golden.

❻ Carefully remove from the oven and allow to cool for a couple of minutes. Use a teaspoon to lift the bites from the tray and lay onto a serving plate. Sprinkle with chives and black pepper.

Orange and lemon pilaf with pistachios

I love a sharing plate of pilaf – fragrant, fresh, and a great way to use up some post-Christmas citrus fruits. Choose white basmati rice for the quickest cooking time and the best fragrance. Although I've included this in the leftovers chapter, I have been known to make and serve this at festive 'bring and share' lunches, buffets and parties. Serve either hot or cold.

Serves 4

1 tbsp sunflower oil

1 onion, chopped

1 tsp ground turmeric

½ tsp ground cumin

pinch of chilli flakes

1 tsp harissa paste

250g (1¼ cups) white basmati rice

800ml (3⅓ cups) hot vegetable stock

4 tbsp shelled pistachios, roughly chopped

zest and juice of 1 unwaxed lemon

zest and juice of ½ unwaxed orange

generous handful of flat-leaf parsley, finely chopped

generous pinch each of sea salt and black pepper

Easy tip

Adding the lemon and orange juice and zest at the end of cooking stops any unwanted bitter flavours developing, and brings true freshness and flavour to the pilaf.

❶ Add the oil and onion to a large pan, then cook the onion over a medium-high heat for 3–5 minutes until softened but not browned. Stir in the turmeric, cumin, chilli flakes and harissa and cook for a further minute.

❷ Pour in the rice and vegetable stock and bring to the boil. Reduce the heat to medium and simmer for 15 minutes, stirring frequently to avoid sticking, until the liquid has been absorbed.

❸ Remove from the heat and use a fork to work through the rice. Place a lid on the pan and allow to stand for 5 minutes.

❹ Meanwhile, add the pistachios to a dry pan and toast over a medium heat for 2–3 minutes until toasted and fragrant.

❺ Stir the lemon and orange zest and juice through the rice, then stir in the parsley until evenly distributed.

❻ Season to taste with salt and pepper, then scatter over the toasted pistachios.

Boxing Day balti

It's that day of the year to use up all the leftovers, and this curry is my favourite way to do it. Adding a spoonful of cranberry sauce during cooking reduces any acidic flavour from the passata, and gives a gentle fruity flavour, similar to mango chutney. Serve with fluffy basmati rice or warmed vegan naan breads.

Serves 4
Suitable for freezing

1 tbsp sunflower oil
1 onion, finely diced
2 garlic cloves, crushed
1 tsp ground cumin
1 tsp ground turmeric
generous pinch of dried chilli flakes
2 rounded tbsp medium curry paste
    (ensure vegan)
500g (2 cups/17oz) passata (sieved
    tomatoes)
1 tbsp cranberry sauce
1 tray of leftover roasted vegetables
juice of ½ unwaxed lemon
generous pinch of sea salt
generous handful of fresh coriander
    (cilantro), roughly torn

1 In a large pan, heat the oil and onion over a high heat for 3–4 minutes until the onion begins to soften. Add the garlic, cumin, turmeric and chilli flakes and cook for 1 minute.

2 Add the curry paste, passata and cranberry sauce, then bring to the boil and simmer for 10 minutes, stirring occasionally.

3 Spoon in the leftover roasted vegetables and heat through for 2–3 minutes. Remove from the heat and stir in the lemon juice. Season to taste with sea salt.

4 Scatter with fresh coriander just before serving.

Easy tip
Put out a bowl of coconut yogurt for guests to swirl through the curry, to take the edge off the spices.

Anything-goes bhajis with coconut raita

I can't get enough of freshly fried bhajis. There's just something about their crisp, hot crunch that is comforting and satisfying, especially when dipped into a cooling raita. This version uses up all the vegetables left over from Christmas day; some of my favourites include shredded sprouts, cauliflower, green beans and spinach. Or keep it simple with classic onion bhajis. Use up what you have!

Serves 4

1 carrot, peeled and grated

1 parsnip, peeled and grated

few florets of broccoli, finely chopped

1 red onion, thinly sliced

1 tsp garam masala

1 tsp mild chilli powder

pinch of chilli flakes

5 rounded tbsp plain (all-purpose) flour

200ml (generous ¾ cup) sunflower oil, for frying

4 rounded tbsp thick coconut yogurt, chilled

small handful of fresh mint leaves, finely chopped

pinch of sea salt

juice of ¼ unwaxed lemon

Easy tip

Aim for one small bowlful of grated and chopped vegetables per batch, or simply increase the spice, flour and water ratio to suit.

❶ In a large bowl, combine the carrot, parsnip, broccoli and red onion.

❷ Stir in the garam masala, chilli powder and chilli flakes, then stir in the flour. Pour in 80ml (⅓ cup) cold water and stir to form a thick batter. Combine fully to ensure all of the vegetables are coated.

❸ Heat the oil in a pan over a medium-high heat until hot. Test if the oil is hot enough for frying by dropping in a small amount of batter; if it rises to the top and becomes golden, the oil is hot enough. Add tablespoon-sized amounts of the mixture to the pan, 2–3 at a time, so you don't overcrowd the pan (which can lead to them sticking together).

❹ Remove the bhajis from the pan and drain on kitchen paper. Keep warm until all of the bhajis are cooked.

❺ To make the coconut raita, stir together the coconut yogurt and mint. Season with the pinch of sea salt.

❻ Squeeze the lemon juice over the hot bhajis, then serve with the raita.

Mac and leftovers

Everyone loves a comforting mac and cheese – and this version combines leftover root vegetables with vegan cheese to create a smooth and satisfying sauce. Stir through macaroni, or your favourite pasta, for a warming family meal.

Serves 4

3 carrots, peeled and roughly chopped

1 sweet potato, peeled and roughly chopped

1 large baking potato, peeled and roughly chopped

½ butternut squash, peeled and roughly chopped

400g (14oz) dried macaroni (ensure egg-free)

1 tsp dried sage

200ml (generous ¾ cup) unsweetened soya milk

100g (3½oz) vegan hard cheese, grated

generous handful of fresh chives, finely chopped

generous pinch each of sea salt and black pepper

❶ Bring a large pan of water to the boil over a medium heat, then throw in the chopped carrots, sweet potato, potato and butternut squash. Simmer for 20 minutes until the vegetables have softened, the drain away the water.

❷ Meanwhile, bring another pan of water to the boil and throw in the macaroni. Cook for 10–12 minutes until al dente, then drain away the water. Return the cooked macaroni to the pan.

❸ Add the cooked carrot, potato and squash to a high-powered jug blender and spoon in the sage. Pour in the soya milk and vegan cheese, then blitz until completely smooth.

❹ Pour the sauce over the macaroni and stir through over a medium heat.

❺ Remove from the heat and stir in the chives. Season to taste with salt and pepper and serve hot.

Easy tip

The root vegetable sauce is suitable for freezing before the vegan cheese is added, so whip up a batch and freeze it, then simply add the cheese when reheating before stirring through freshly cooked macaroni.

Stir-fried sprouts with edamame, ginger and chilli

For when you need something fresh and light after Christmas – and a perfect excuse to use up all of those sprouts! Canned water chestnuts can be found in most supermarkets – check the world food aisle. They're also a perfect addition to sweet and sour dishes and Chinese-style curries. Serve with steamed rice and crispy tofu, if you like.

Serves 4

1 tbsp sunflower oil

2cm (¾in) piece of ginger, peeled and grated

1 fresh red chilli, deseeded and finely chopped

200g (7oz) Brussels sprouts, finely shredded

225g (8oz) can of water chestnuts, drained and rinsed

4 rounded tbsp frozen or fresh edamame beans

2 tbsp sesame seeds

2 tbsp light soy sauce

2 spring onions (scallions), finely chopped

small handful of fresh coriander (cilantro), roughly torn

Easy tip

If you don't have quite enough leftover sprouts, 'bulk' the dish up with shredded cabbage, kale or ribboned carrots.

---

❶ Heat the oil in a wok over a high heat. When hot, throw in the ginger and chilli and stir-fry for a few seconds until the oil is infused.

❷ Add the sprouts, then stir-fry for 2–3 minutes until they begin to soften. Add the water chestnuts, edamame beans, sesame seeds and soy sauce and stir-fry for a further 2 minutes.

❸ Remove from the heat and stir in the spring onions. Top with coriander just before serving.

Fig, mushroom and red onion roaster

Roasting pan suppers are the answer to your prayers in that week between Christmas and New Year celebrations, when you don't really have the inclination to cook. I love including sweet and jammy figs, to balance the earthy flavour of the mushrooms, sage and nuts.

Serves 4

1 garlic clove, bruised

250g (9oz) chestnut (cremini) mushrooms, brushed clean and halved

2 sweet potatoes, peeled and diced

2 red onions, chopped

4 figs, quartered

drizzle of sunflower oil

pinch of dried sage

2 sprigs of fresh rosemary

2 tbsp pine nuts

small handful of flat-leaf parsley, finely chopped

2 rounded tbsp unsweetened plain soya yogurt

generous pinch each of sea salt and black pepper

Easy tip

If you have any leftover ultimate vegan gravy (page 106), switch the yogurt for this, for a comforting supper.

1 Preheat the oven to 190°C/375°F/gas mark 5.

2 Rub the garlic clove over a deep roasting tray to release the fragrance, then discard.

3 Add the mushrooms, sweet potatoes, red onions and figs to the roasting tray. Drizzle with sunflower oil and stir to lightly coat the vegetables. Sprinkle over the sage, and lay in the whole rosemary sprigs. Roast in the oven for 20 minutes.

4 Carefully remove from the oven and scatter over the pine nuts. Return to the oven for a further 5 minutes until the pine nuts are golden and toasted.

5 Remove from the oven and stir through the parsley. Spoon over the yogurt, then season to taste with salt and plenty of pepper.

Winter apple slaw

Maple and mustard balance the fresh and zingy flavours of this slaw, which is perfect for using up those leftover veggies at the back of the fridge. Perfect when served with lunch during those long days between Christmas and New Year.

Serves 4

2 Granny Smith apples, cored
   and sliced into thin wedges
2 carrots, peeled and grated
½ red cabbage, shredded
1 celery stick, thinly sliced
½ small red onion, chopped
1 tbsp dried cranberries
1 tbsp maple syrup
6 rounded tbsp vegan mayonnaise
1 tsp Dijon mustard

Easy tip

Granny Smith apples deliver on crunch, freshness and colour, but if you don't have any available Braeburn or Cox apples are excellent alternatives.

❶ Toss the apples, carrots, cabbage, celery, red onion and dried cranberries into a large bowl.

❷ Stir in the maple syrup, mayonnaise and mustard until all of the vegetables are evenly coated. The slaw will keep for up to 2 days, covered, in the fridge.

Drinks

Slow cooker gingerbread latte

Make the perfect after-dinner gingerbread latte in your slow cooker, to simmer and infuse while you enjoy your meal. And I'll let you into a secret: it's not just for after dinner. I love drinking it throughout December, especially while I'm wrapping the gifts! Sweet, spicy and full of festive cheer.

Serves 4

200ml (generous ¾ cup) freshly brewed good-quality espresso coffee (about 4 shots)

800ml (3⅓ cups) oat milk

1 tbsp black treacle

1 tbsp golden syrup

1 rounded tsp ground ginger

½ tsp ground cinnamon

½ tsp grated nutmeg

pinch of ground allspice

vegan canned 'squirty' cream, to serve

sprinkle of golden caster (superfine) sugar, to serve

Easy tip

Black treacle gives the latte an extra flavour layer, just like it does in gingerbread. Use up the rest of your tin for sticky gingerbread pudding with salted caramel sauce (page 161).

❶ Pour the coffee and oat milk into a slow cooker, then add the treacle, golden syrup, ginger, cinnamon, nutmeg and allspice.

❷ Set the slow cooker on the low setting for 2 hours.

❸ Stir thoroughly, then pour or ladle into coffee cups or mugs. Swirl over the vegan canned cream, and sprinkle with caster sugar.

Christmas morning tea

If you've had the early morning wake-up by the little ones, and it's now an excited and frantic race to unwrap the presents under the tree, take a moment of calm with this milky and indulgent spiced latte tea.

Serves 4

800ml (3⅓ cups) oat milk

6 rounded tbsp good-quality loose
    English breakfast tea

2 tsp soft light brown sugar

8 cardamom pods, cracked

3 cloves

1 cinnamon stick

generous pinch of grated nutmeg

Easy tip

Prepare the spices and place them into a sealed tub on Christmas Eve, ready to throw into the pan come Christmas morning.

❶ Pour the oat milk into a pan and heat over a low heat until very gently simmering (but not boiling).

❷ Stir in the tea, sugar, cardamom pods, cloves, cinnamon and nutmeg and simmer over a low heat for 10 minutes to infuse.

❸ Pour through a tea strainer or sieve into mugs.

No-egg nog

Creamy, boozy and gently spiced, this rich beverage will step you into Christmas. Feel free to top with some vegan whipped cream, but I like to keep it simple with a generous sprinkling of nutmeg. This no-egg nog is equally as delicious without the alcohol.

Serves 4

1 x 400ml (14fl oz) can of full-fat
  coconut milk
200ml (generous ¾ cup) almond milk,
  chilled
1 tsp good-quality vanilla extract
5 generous tbsp maple syrup
generous pinch of ground cinnamon
generous pinch of freshly grated nutmeg,
  plus extra to serve
pinch of ground cardamom
4 measures of amaretto

Easy tip

Switch the amaretto for rum or whisky, or your favourite spirit, to personalize the drink to your taste.

---

❶ In a high-powered jug blender, blitz together the coconut milk and almond milk until frothy.

❷ Add the vanilla extract, maple syrup, cinnamon, nutmeg, cardamom and amaretto, then blitz again until combined.

❸ Pour into chilled glasses, then top with a little extra grated nutmeg.

Cranberry mimosas

Mimosas are the perfect way to start the day, and this Christmas edition switches orange juice for cranberry juice. Pop in a couple of frozen cranberries for decoration (and to keep the drinks cool), or garnish with wedges of orange or pink grapefuit.

Serves 4

12 tbsp sweetened cranberry juice
½ unwaxed orange
4 sprigs of fresh thyme
chilled champagne, to top (ensure vegan)

❶ Lay out four champagne glasses, and pour 3 tablespoons cranberry juice into each.

❷ Squeeze a little orange juice into each glass, then muddle with the thyme sprig, and leave one in each glass.

❸ Top with champagne just before serving.

Easy tip

Many brands of champagne are vegan friendly, although some do contain animal ingredients such as isinglass, so be sure to check before purchasing. Vegan prosecco makes a good alternative.

Pomegranate and rosemary punch

A grown-up Christmas punch, without any alcohol. This long drink has plenty of bitter and zesty flavours, alongside wintery rosemary for fragrance.

Serves 4 generously

1 litre (4 cups) pomegranate juice
4 sprigs of fresh rosemary
½ unwaxed grapefruit, sliced
½ unwaxed orange, sliced
500ml (2 cups) sparkling tonic water, chilled
ice, to serve

Easy tip

Bottles of pomegranate juice can be purchased in supermarkets – there's no need to juice fresh pomegranates to make this punch!

---

❶ In a large punch bowl or jug, combine the pomegranate juice, rosemary sprigs and grapefruit and orange slices. Refrigerate for 1–2 hours to allow to infuse.

❷ Pour in the tonic water just before serving. Stir through to combine evenly.

❸ Ladle or pour into chilled glasses, over ice if you like.

Spiced clementine cordial

Whether you're looking to make a homemade gift for a loved one, or are simply using up all those ripe clementines, this cordial is easy to make and delicious to drink. Serve to taste with chilled sparkling water and ice, or with a splash of cloudy lemonade.

Serves 4 generously

500g (1lb 2oz) clementines, halved

200ml (generous ¾ cup) sweetened
    cranberry juice

300g (1½ cups) caster (superfine) sugar

pared zest of 1 unwaxed lemon

1 cinnamon stick

1 bay leaf

2 star anise

Easy tip

This cordial will keep for up to 2 weeks in a sealed, sterilized jar or bottle, when kept in the fridge.

---

1 Squeeze the juice of the clementines into a pan, adding a few pieces of the rind.

2 Pour in the cranberry juice, along with 150ml (5fl oz) cold water. Stir in the sugar.

3 Bring to the boil over a high heat, then once boiling, add the lemon zest, cinnamon, bay leaf and star anise. Reduce the heat to low and simmer lightly for 50–60 minutes until it reduces to a light syrup.

4 Remove from the heat and allow to cool fully.

5 Pour through a sieve into a sterilized jar or bottle.

Mulled wine

I like to let my slow cooker do all of the hard work here, while I get on with better things! Use the 'keep warm' function on your slow cooker if you're serving mulled wine for a party or gathering, to save you reheating.

Pictured on page 14.

Serves 4

1 bottle of red wine (ensure vegan;
   see page 15)
2 tbsp maple syrup
2 cinnamon sticks
4 cloves
2 star anise
1 unwaxed orange, thinly sliced
½ unwaxed lemon, thinly sliced

❶ Add all of the ingredients to a slow cooker and cook on the low setting for 2 hours. Alternatively, add everything to a heavy-based saucepan and warm over a low heat for 10 minutes.

❷ Ladle into heatproof glass mugs to serve.

> **Easy tip**
> This mulled wine can also be made in a large pan – simply simmer all of the ingredients over a medium heat (without boiling) for 8–10 minutes until fragrant.

Candy cane hot chocolate

After a long day of Christmas shopping, kick back and relax with this sweet, minty hot chocolate. I like to use oat milk to make hot chocolate, as it is naturally smooth and thick, but feel free to use your favourite plant-based milk. If you don't have any mint dark chocolate available, simply add ½ teaspoon good-quality peppermint flavouring to the pan with the milk.

Serves 4

500ml (2 cups) oat milk

200g (7oz) mint dark chocolate (ensure vegan), broken into even pieces

100ml (scant ½ cup) vegan double (heavy) cream

4 candy canes (ensure vegan; see Easy Tip)

Easy tip

Ensure you read the ingredients of the candy canes for any hidden animal ingredients, such as the red colouring carmine or cochineal. Many supermarket brands of candy cane use vegan-friendly colours, with clear labelling on the packaging.

❶ Heat the oat milk in a pan over a low-medium heat. Once hot – but not boiling – add the chocolate and gently stir until it is melted.

❷ Stir in the cream until combined.

❸ Pour into mugs. Place a candy cane in each mug, and stir, allowing the candy cane to gently melt into the drink as it is being enjoyed.

Festive Bakes & Treats

Ten-minute figgy pudding

If you've missed 'Stir-up Sunday', or need to prepare a pudding in a hurry, this speedy take on a traditional Christmas pudding is easy, fast and delicious. This pudding is cooked in the microwave, so there's no need to steam it for hours. Serve with brandy butter (page 119), vegan pouring cream or vegan custard.

Serves 4–6
Suitable for freezing

100ml (scant ½ cup) soya milk

1 tsp cider vinegar

100g (scant ½ cup) vegan butter

100g (½ cup) soft dark brown sugar

100g (scant 1 cup) self-raising flour

2 tsp ground allspice

1 tsp grated nutmeg

2 tbsp maple syrup

1 rounded tbsp shop-bought
   cranberry sauce

1 apple, grated

100g (3½oz) dried figs, roughly chopped

100g (3½oz) raisins

100g (3½oz) sultanas (golden raisins)

Easy tip

Pop this pudding in the microwave while you're having your Christmas dinner, then allow it cool in the bowl for 10–12 minutes after cooking to keep its traditional 'pudding' shape, or cook it the day before and simply reheat as needed.

1 Pour the soya milk into a jug and stir in the cider vinegar. Allow to curdle for a few minutes to form a buttermilk.

2 Meanwhile, add the butter and sugar to a bowl and whisk until light and fluffy.

3 Fold in the flour, allspice, nutmeg, maple syrup and cranberry sauce. Pour in the buttermilk mixture and stir to combine.

4 Fold in the apple, figs, raisins and sultanas until fully coated in the mix.

5 Pour the mix into a 1.2-litre (2-pint) pudding basin or heatproof bowl and cover the top loosely with baking parchment. Cook in a 900W microwave for 10 minutes, then allow to stand for 10–12 minutes.

6 Carefully tip out onto a plate. Serve with vegan brandy butter or vegan cream, or ladle over flaming brandy.

Sticky gingerbread pudding with salted caramel sauce

Not everybody loves a currant-infused Christmas pudding. This festive twist on a sticky toffee pudding makes an excellent alternative, complete with a rich sauce for pouring.

Serves 4 generously
Suitable for freezing

For the gingerbread pudding
150g (1¼ cups) plain (all-purpose) flour
1 tsp baking powder
½ tsp bicarbonate of soda (baking soda)
3 tsp ground ginger
1 tsp grated nutmeg
1 tsp mixed spice (pumpkin pie spice)
1 tsp ground cinnamon
2 rounded tbsp black treacle
2 rounded tbsp golden syrup
50ml (scant ¼ cup) soya or oat milk
120ml (½ cup) sunflower oil
2 tbsp vanilla soya yogurt

For the sauce
3 tbsp soft light brown sugar
2 rounded tbsp golden syrup
1 rounded tbsp vegan butter
1 tsp good-quality vanilla extract
½ tsp sea salt, plus extra for sprinkling
250ml (1 cup) vegan double (heavy)
   cream

❶ Preheat the oven to 180°C/350°F/gas mark 4.

❷ Mix the flour, baking powder, bicarbonate of soda, ginger, nutmeg, mixed spice and cinnamon in a bowl.

❸ In a separate bowl, whisk together the black treacle, golden syrup, soya milk, sunflower oil and soya yogurt until combined. Pour the dry ingredients into the wet mixture and stir together until just combined.

❹ Pour into a 20cm (8in) brownie tin and bake in the oven for 25–30 minutes. Allow to cool before slicing into 8 squares.

❺ To make the salted caramel sauce, melt the sugar, golden syrup, vegan butter, vanilla extract and sea salt in a pan over a low heat for 5–6 minutes, without stirring, until it bubbles. Remove from the heat and allow to cool for a few minutes. Whisk in the cream until combined and smooth.

❻ Place a couple of squares per serving bowl, then generously pour over the sauce.

Easy tip

Both the cake and the sauce can be prepared in advance and frozen. Freeze in separate containers, defrost and reheat thoroughly, then pour over the sauce just before serving.

Toasted coconut and marshmallow panna cotta

This fun and flirty dessert combines marshmallows, a creamy panna cotta, and crisp toasted coconut. If you don't have traditional dariole moulds, small tumblers make a good alternative.

Serves 4

1 x 400ml (14fl oz) can of full-fat
  coconut milk
2 tbsp caster (superfine) sugar
1 tsp vanilla extract
2 tsp agar agar flakes
2 rounded tbsp flaked coconut
50g (1¾oz) pink and white vegan
  marshmallows, torn into small chunks,
  plus a few for garnish

Easy tip

Gelatine- and carmine-free marshmallows are available in supermarkets, and are clearly labelled as vegan. When heating the marshmallows, ensure you use a large pan over a low heat as they will expand and melt, and may splatter very hot sugar solution, so be careful at this stage.

1 Add the coconut milk, sugar, vanilla extract and agar agar flakes to a pan and bring to a simmer over a medium heat for 5–6 minutes until the agar agar flakes have fully dissolved.

2 Pour the mixture into four small dariole moulds, then refrigerate overnight, or for at least 8 hours, until set but still a little wobbly.

3 Up to 15 minutes before serving dessert, add the flaked coconut to a dry pan and toast over a medium heat for 2–3 minutes until golden and fragrant. Tip the toasted coconut onto a plate and set aside. Using the same pan, add the marshmallows and begin to melt over a low heat. Stir occasionally to encourage even melting, but be careful, as the high-sugar mixture can get very hot very quickly.

4 Remove the panna cotta from the fridge and allow to stand for a few minutes to make removal easier. Place the moulds on plates and gently shake to remove the panna cotta.

5 Carefully toast a few reserved marshmallows under a medium grill (broiler) on a baking sheet lined with foil. Keep on eye on them as they will toast very quickly!

6 Just before serving, spoon the hot marshmallow onto the plate next to the panna cotta, scatter with the toasted coconut and garnish with a couple of toasted marshmallows per plate.

Limoncello mousse

After a delicious roast dinner, this is the perfect zesty and creamy dessert. Italian limoncello adds a clean zing, which is delicious with the flavours of vegan white chocolate and vanilla. Feel free to top with winter berries, or a crumbled vegan caramel biscuit, for texture.

Serves 4

340g (12oz) silken tofu
200g (7oz) vegan white chocolate,
   broken into even pieces
1 tsp good-quality vanilla extract
4 tbsp limoncello
finely grated zest of 2 unwaxed lemons

Easy tip

Silken tofu gives the smooth base to this dessert. It has a naturally creamy texture, unlike firm tofu. You'll find silken tofu in world food aisles, often stored ambient rather than chilled.

1 Add the silken tofu to a high-powered jug blender and blitz on high until smooth, or use a stick blender to blitz the silken tofu in a bowl.

2 Add the white chocolate to a heatproof bowl, then melt over a pan of boiling water, making sure the base of the bowl does not touch the water. Stir occasionally until the chocolate has melted into a shiny liquid, then carefully pour into the blended tofu.

3 Stir in the vanilla extract and limoncello, then blitz again to ensure the mixture is silky smooth and fully combined.

4 Stir in the lemon zest then spoon into four ramekin dishes. Chill in the fridge for at least 4 hours, or overnight, until set.

Easy rich chocolate torte

This decadent chocolate torte uses store-cupboard ingredients to create a luxurious dessert. Vacuum-packed chestnuts are blitzed into a smooth paste before being combined with dark chocolate, and a pinch of flaky sea salt. Prepare in advance, then slice just before serving for best results.

Serves 6

2 tsp amaretto

125g (½ cup) vegan butter

100g (generous ¾ cup) icing (confectioners') sugar, plus extra for dusting

pinch of sea salt

200g (7oz) good-quality dark chocolate (ensure vegan), broken into even squares

180g (6oz) vacuum-packed chestnuts

1 tsp cocoa powder, for dusting

To serve (all optional)

edible gold leaf

1 or 2 clementines, peeled and sliced into rounds

vegan whipping cream, whipped to soft peaks

dark chocolate, grated (ensure vegan)

Easy tip

For easy serving, rinse a sharp knife under hot water between slicing each portion.

❶ Line a small 450g (1lb) loaf tin with cling film (plastic wrap), ensuring there is overhang.

❷ In bowl, stir together the amaretto, vegan butter, icing sugar and salt. Use an electric whisk to beat until light and fluffy.

❸ Bring a pan of water to a simmer and set a heatproof bowl over it, making sure the base does not touch the water beneath. Add the chocolate to the bowl and allow to melt fully, then leave to cool for a few minutes.

❹ Meanwhile, add the chestnuts to a high-powered jug blender or food processor and blitz until they become a thick, smooth paste.

❺ Stir the melted chocolate and chestnut paste into the beaten butter and sugar mix. Spoon into the lined loaf tin, cover with the overhanging cling film, then allow to chill overnight, or for at least 8–10 hours.

❻ Remove the set torte from the fridge and carefully turn out onto a clean surface. Dust with icing sugar and cocoa powder. Slice just before serving (see Easy Tip).

❼ This is delicious served on its own, but I love to elevate it with any or all of the following. Press a little gold leaf onto each slice, then garnish with a slice of clementine, a dollop of cream and scatter over chocolate shavings, before serving.

Gingerbread and maple pancakes

Not only are these spiced pancakes delicious as a special breakfast, but they also make a wonderful dessert that requires very little effort. Serve with a generous drizzle of maple syrup and a sprinkle of unwaxed lemon zest to really make the gingerbread flavour pop. These are also delicious served with toasted pecans, cherries in syrup and a scoop of ice cream, if you like.

Makes 6

100g (scant 1 cup) plain (all-purpose) flour

½ tsp ground ginger

½ tsp ground cinnamon

pinch of grated nutmeg

pinch of salt

200ml (generous ¾ cup) sweetened soya milk, chilled

6 tbsp sunflower oil, for frying

generous drizzle of good-quality maple syrup

zest of ½ unwaxed lemon

Easy tip

Chill the pancake batter in the fridge overnight, or for at least 4 hours, to rest and thicken.

❶ In a large bowl, stir together the flour, ginger, cinnamon, nutmeg and salt until combined. Pour in the soya milk and whisk to create a smooth batter. Refrigerate overnight, or for at least 4 hours.

❷ Add 1 tablespoon of the sunflower oil to a pancake pan and set over a medium-high heat. Test if the oil is hot by dripping a small amount of the chilled mixture into the pan; if it sizzles and becomes golden within 20 seconds, it is at the right temperature. Swirl in 4 tablespoons of the batter and cook for 2–3 minutes, then flip the pancake over and cook the other side.

❸ Transfer to a plate lined with kitchen paper and keep warm while you repeat the process, using 1 tbsp of sunflower oil per pancake.

❹ Drizzle the pancakes with maple syrup and scatter with lemon zest just before serving, or put on the table for people to help themselves.

Traditional Christmas cake

Nothing beats cutting that first slice of homemade Christmas cake: plump fruit, spices, brown sugar and marzipan, finished with smooth icing. Although it may initially seem complicated, it's actually a simple cake to bake. Always soak the dried fruit overnight until plump; I love to use fresh orange juice for this, as it infuses the cake with a zesty flavour to lift the richness. This cake is equally as delicious served naked, without marzipan or icing; if you prefer this simplicity, press a few blanched almonds over the top for the final 30 minutes of baking.

Serves 8–10
Suitable for freezing without marzipan and icing)

300g (10oz) sultanas (golden raisins)
250g (9oz) raisins
200g (7oz) glacé cherries
100g (3½oz) dried mixed (candied) peel
600ml (2½ cups) fresh orange juice
300ml (1¼ cups) soya milk
2 tsp cider vinegar
300g (2½ cups) self-raising flour
1 tsp baking powder
pinch of salt
1 tsp ground cinnamon
1 tsp grated nutmeg
1 tsp ground allspice
1 tsp ground ginger
100g (scant ½ cup) vegan butter
200g (1 cup) soft dark brown sugar
brandy, rum or whisky for feeding
   (ensure vegan)
2 tbsp apricot jam
450g (1lb) shop-bought golden marzipan
   (ensure vegan)
500g (1lb 2oz) shop-bought ready-to-roll
   icing (ensure vegan)

❶ Add the sultanas, raisins, cherries and mixed peel to a large bowl and pour over the orange juice. Soak for at least 1 hour or overnight, then drain away the orange juice.

❷ Preheat the oven to 180°C/350°F/gas mark 4 and line an 18cm (7in) cake tin with baking parchment.

❸ Pour the soya milk into a jug and stir in the cider vinegar. Allow to stand for a few minutes to curdle and become a buttermilk.

❹ In a large bowl, stir together the flour, baking powder, salt, cinnamon, nutmeg, allspice and ginger. Rub in the vegan butter, until the mixture resembles breadcrumbs.

❺ Stir in the sugar, then fold in the buttermilk and mix to form a batter, then add the pre-soaked fruit, stirring to fully coat in the batter. Tip the mixture into the lined cake tin and bake in the oven for 45 minutes.

❻ After 45 minutes, reduce the heat to 160°C/325°F/gas mark 3 and bake the cake for a further hour, until a cake skewer comes out clean.

❼ Once removed from the oven, prick the top of the cake all over with a fork, then allow to cool fully before removing from the cake tin.

❽ If you're feeding the cake with brandy, rum or whisky, spoon over 1–2 tablespoons initially once the cake is cool, then wrap in baking parchment and keep in a container in a cool place. Feed the cake once a week for 4–6 weeks.

❾ When you are ready to ice the cake, brush the top and sides of the cake with the apricot jam. Roll out the marzipan and smooth it onto the cake, pressing neatly around the sides and trimming away the excess. Roll out the icing and smooth onto the cake in the same way. Finish with any other festive decorations, and a ribbon around the base, if you like.

Easy tip

If you're planning to 'feed' the cake with alcohol for a boozy flavour and longer life, bake it 4–6 weeks before Christmas. If you wish to enjoy the cake without the alcohol, bake it 3–7 days before eating.

Mince pie Danish pastries

If you're looking for an excuse to eat mince pies for breakfast, this is the recipe for you! Switch up the traditional shortcrust pastry for puff pastry to turn the classic ingredients into a pastry treat that is perfect for breakfast, with a mid-morning coffee, or as a warming snack after carol singing.

Makes 12

1 sheet of ready-rolled puff pastry
    (ensure vegan; see page 15)
4 rounded tbsp jarred mincemeat
    (ensure vegan)
1 tbsp dried cranberries
1 tsp blanched chopped hazelnuts
finely grated zest of 1 unwaxed orange
1 tsp soya milk, for glazing
2 tbsp icing (confectioners') sugar

Easy tip

Most jarred, sweet mincemeat found in supermarkets is suitable for vegans (as vegetable suet is commonly used) but always check the ingredients before you buy.

---

1 Preheat the oven to 200°C/400°F/gas mark 6 and line a baking tray with baking parchment.

2 Unroll the pastry sheet onto a clean surface, then spread the mincemeat evenly over the pastry. Scatter over the cranberries, hazelnuts and orange zest.

3 Starting at a shorter end of the pastry, firmly roll the pastry to the other side, to form a full roll. Slice the roll into 12 pieces, then place on the baking tray.

4 Brush with the soya milk, then bake in the oven for 12–15 minutes until golden.

5 Meanwhile mix the icing sugar with 2–3 teaspoons cold water to form a smooth drizzle.

6 Remove the pastries from the oven and allow to cool for a few minutes. Drizzle with the icing. Enjoy warm.

Snow marble cupcakes

These chocolate cupcakes taste as good as they look (and kids will love to get involved in the mixing!). Piping the marble-effect frosting through a star-shaped nozzle gives the best shape; pipe the frosting around the outer edge of the cupcake, moving it inwards and upwards as you go.

Makes 12
Suitable for freezing (before frosting)

For the cupcakes
250ml (1 cup) sweetened soya milk
1 tsp cider vinegar
150g (¾ cup) granulated sugar
100ml (scant ½ cup) sunflower oil
1 tsp good-quality vanilla extract
150g (1¼ cups) plain (all-purpose) flour
50g (½ cup) cocoa powder
¾ tsp bicarbonate of soda (baking soda)
½ tsp baking powder
sprinkles (optional)

For the snow marble buttercream
200g (scant 1 cup) vegan butter,
    at room temperature
450g (3½ cups) icing (confectioners')
    sugar
1 tsp good-quality vanilla extract
1 tsp cocoa powder

Easy tip
For a flavour twist, add 1 teaspoon peppermint, coffee or orange extract to the cake batter.

❶ Preheat the oven to 190°C/375°F/gas mark 5 and line a 12-hole cupcake tray with paper cases.

❷ In a jug, whisk together the soya milk and cider vinegar. Leave to stand for a couple of minutes until it appears thickened. Whisk in the sugar, sunflower oil and vanilla extract.

❸ In a large bowl, stir together the flour, cocoa powder, bicarbonate of soda and baking powder. Pour in the liquid mixture from the jug and fold until just combined.

❹ Spoon the cake batter evenly into the paper cases. Bake in the oven for 18–20 minutes until springy to the touch and slightly shiny on the top. Allow to cool fully.

❺ For the buttercream, add the vegan butter to a large bowl and fork through until softened.

❻ Stir in half of the icing sugar and mix with a wooden spoon until combined. Pour in the remaining half and fold in to form a stiff mixture. Spoon in the vanilla extract, then use an electric whisk to beat for 4–5 minutes until light and paler in colour.

❼ Prepare a piping bag with a star-shaped nozzle. Spoon half of the buttercream into one side of the piping bag and set aside.

❽ Stir the cocoa powder into the remaining buttercream in the bowl. Whisk until fully combined, then spoon into the other side of the piping bag, so the vanilla and chocolate buttercreams run vertically with each other.

❾ Swirl the marble-effect buttercream onto the cooled cupcakes then top with sprinkles, if you like. Enjoy within 2–3 days.

Chocolate orange millionaire's shortbread

It's not a celebration without a square (or two) of millionaire's shortbread, and this festive edition has the nostalgic Christmas flavours of chocolate orange. The crumbly, buttery base is topped with a smooth caramel, and a layer of orange-infused chocolate. These squares will last for up to a week when stored in a sealed container.

Makes about 15

For the biscuit base
250g (2 cups) plain (all-purpose) flour
pinch of sea salt
200g (scant 1 cup) vegan butter, chilled
100g (½ cup) caster (superfine) sugar

For the caramel sauce
1 x 370g (13oz) can of vegan condensed milk
1 tbsp vegan butter
2 tbsp soft light brown sugar
1 tsp vanilla extract

For the chocolate topping
200g (7oz) dark chocolate (ensure vegan), broken into even pieces
finely grated zest of 1 unwaxed orange, finely grated

1 Preheat the oven to 160°C/325°F/gas mark 3 and line a 20 x 30cm (8 x 12in) baking tin with baking parchment.

2 Combine the flour and salt in a large bowl. Break up the vegan butter and rub it into the flour until it resembles breadcrumbs, then stir in the sugar until fully combined.

3 Press the mixture into the lined baking tray, smoothing it with the back of a spoon. Bake in the oven for 40–45 minutes, then allow to cool fully.

4 To make the caramel sauce, add the vegan condensed milk, vegan butter, sugar and vanilla extract to a pan and place over a low heat. Gradually bring to a simmer, then remove from the heat. Use a balloon whisk to beat the mixture for 5–6 minutes until thickened. Allow to cool for a few minutes, then pour and smooth over the biscuit base. Allow to cool completely.

5 Bring a pan of water to the boil over a medium heat and set a heatproof bowl over the top, making sure the base does not touch the water beneath. Add the chocolate and allow it to melt fully, then remove from the heat and stir in the orange zest. Pour over the caramel and allow to cool and set completely, before slicing into squares.

Easy tip

Cans of vegan condensed milk are now available in large supermarkets and in health-food stores. Some brands use a rice and oat base, where some use a coconut milk base. These alternatives can successfully replace dairy condensed milk in recipes.

Rudolph's cherry and pretzel chocolate bark

This fun recipe is a great way to get children involved in baking over the Christmas holidays. This easy chocolate bark is delicious as a Christmas Eve treat, or to bag up as a homemade gift for a loved one. Once broken into shards, it will last for up to 2 weeks in a sealed container.

Serves 4–6

200g (7oz) good-quality dark chocolate (ensure vegan)
50g (1¾oz) vegan white chocolate
4 generous handfuls of salted pretzels
100g (3½oz) glacé cherries, halved

Easy tip

Vegan white chocolate is available in supermarkets, often found in the free-from aisles, in either bar or button form.

---

1 Bring two pans of water to the boil, then reduce to a simmer. Break the dark chocolate evenly into one heatproof bowl, and the white chocolate into another.

2 Place a bowl over each pan, making sure the base of each one does not touch the water below. Allow the chocolate to melt fully, then set aside to cool for a few minutes.

3 Line a baking tray with baking parchment. Pour the dark chocolate over the parchment, spreading it with a spatula to reach the corners.

4 Drizzle over the melted white chocolate and use a skewer, or spoon handle to create swirls and patterns.

5 Scatter over the pretzels and cherries. Allow to set in a cool place (but not the fridge) until hardened.

6 Break the bark into randomly shaped shards.

Index

Thanks

I love Christmas, and have always wanted to put together a collection of my favourite seasonal recipes, so it feels fitting that my tenth book is a celebration of food and festivities.

Firstly, I'd like to thank the editorial team at Quadrille. Heartfelt thanks to commissioning editor Harriet Webster for believing in the project, and for your passion and attention to detail. I love working with you! Thank you to publishing director Sarah Lavelle for the opportunity to write ten beautiful books with Quadrille. Special thanks to copy editor Clare Sayer for the editorial support.

A big thank you to designer Emily Lapworth for the vision, art direction and book design. You get it right every time (especially with a pink cover).

Thank you to photographer Luke Albert, food stylist Tamara Vos and assistant Charlotte Whatcott, and prop stylist Louie Waller for the wonderful photography and styling at The Flower Factory and Studio Boardroom. The shoots are always full of creativity, fun and laughs – I can't wait for the next!

Heartfelt thanks to senior publicity manager Rebecca Smedley for another round of publicity and opportunities. Thank you to the marketing team at Quadrille for your ongoing expertise and advice.

I am so grateful for my wonderful literary agent and friend Victoria Hobbs, and the hardworking team at A.M. Heath. Thank you for believing in me, and for your dedication to authors.

Massive thanks to my wonderful mum and dad, who happily ate Christmas dinners for 6 months while I was testing this book. Thank you for cooking the actual Christmas dinner this year! Thank you to my sister Carolyne and brother-in-law Mark for your support and love. Special thanks to my lovely twin nieces Tamzin and Tara, who are never far from the kitchen themselves. Thank you to Auntie May for your ongoing encouragement. And not forgetting Pandi, the house rabbit, who brings joy and happiness each day.

Thank you to my wonderful readers, who have shown loyalty from the start. I write every recipe with you at the forefront of my mind, for delicious, fuss-free food for every occasion.

First published in 2023 by Quadrille,
an imprint of Hardie Grant Publishing

Quadrille
52–54 Southwark Street
London SE1 1UN
quadrille.com

Cataloguing in Publication Data: a
catalogue record for this book is available
from the British Library.

ISBN: 978 1 78713 945 9

Printed in China

FSC
www.fsc.org

MIX
Paper | Supporting
responsible forestry
FSC™ C020056

Managing Director Sarah Lavelle

Commissioning Editor Harriet Webster

Copy Editor Clare Sayer

Art Direction & Design Emily Lapworth

Typesetter Jonathan Baker

Photographer Luke Albert

Food Stylist Tamara Vos

Prop Stylist Louie Waller

Head of Production Stephen Lang

Production Controller Gary Hayes